C0-AQV-058

MAKING DECISIONS ABOUT DIVERSE LEARNERS:

A GUIDE FOR EDUCATORS

Fern Aefsky

EYE ON EDUCATION
6 Depot Way West, Suite 106
Larchmont, N.Y. 10538

Library of Congress Cataloging-in-Publication Data

Aefsky, Fern.
Making decisions about diverse learners : a guide for educators / by Fern Aefsky.
p. cm.
Includes bibliographical references. (p.).
ISBN 1-883001-94-3
1. Special education—United States—Administration. 2. School principals—United States—Handbooks, manuals, etc. I. Title.

LC3981 .A45 2000
371.9'0973—dc21 00-022350

Production services provided by:
ComManagement
1211 Courtland Drive
Raleigh, NC 27604

DEDICATION

This book is dedicated to the educational practitioners and community stakeholders who assist in providing educational opportunities for children. The joys of watching children learn and develop, and the ability of society to work towards a shared support system on behalf of children is a privilege to observe.

I would like to thank the educators who completed surveys for the purpose of gathering data for this book; Monroe-Woodbury. Mt. St. Mary College, and Nova Southeastern University colleagues for their support and insights; my parents, Harold and Selma Heller for their continuous support of my various endeavors; Leslie Politzer for her unwavering friendship; Peggy Hesselgrave and Jane Harkaway for their continued commitment to special education in spite of obstacles placed before them; and my husband, Carl and sons, Sean & Scott, whose endless support enables me to balance the aspects of my family and professional life.

Preface

This book is intended for building level administrators who deal with diversity among students, including those who are classified educationally disabled and their families. Special education programmatic options range from self-contained special education classes to inclusive classes, where students receive special education in the content class. Different types of service create a multitude of building level issues for stakeholders, including district administrators, parents, students, special education teachers and regular education teachers. This book provides information from a practitioner's point of view, focusing on the entire school community, and reflects information gathered from a national perspective, which will assist in understanding decisions made regarding educating all students effectively.

Introduction

It is common for disciplines within an educational community to separate policies and practices according to differences, rather than search for similarities. For example, many attributes of staff development training, building and staff schedules, and programs are looked at by subject area, grade/building levels, student, staff, and community needs. Within each of these areas, however, focus is placed upon concepts of team building, block schedules, diversity, leadership styles, without thought of how these are inter-related and connected to concerns regarding special education services, problems, and solutions.

Building leaders face daily issues within the special education realm that can be explained and understood through "state of the art" concepts in educational leadership. This book attempts to point out these connections through educational research and practice, assisting educators to better understand roles and responsibilities as members of one educational society. When educational leaders incorporate similarities between disciplines, the less likely teachers, parents, or students are to approach systemic problems in a fragmented manner.

This book serves as a reference tool for educational leaders at building level providing a resource addressing many special education issues. This book identifies key concepts of special education under IDEA 1997 in order for the educational community to move toward a progressive, unified approach to dealing with diverse learners and instructors. Legal issues involving eligibility determination, discipline, student entitlement, and the delivery of appropriate special education services in compliance with mandates and building administrators' responsibilities are presented in a tabbed format for easy reference.

Principals and teachers as decision makers need to be "consumers of the eligibility process and data" so that they can be the "experts" explaining information to parents and staff when asked. While evaluators share results with parents, teachers and parents may further question the building administrator. As an educational leader, the ability to share knowledge of data contributes support to the fact that the educational community includes students with disabilities. Many decisions are discussed throughout the eligibility process, and all stakeholders should have input on behalf of the student.

This guide is intended to assist building administrators with decision making in situations of discipline, legal compliance, and instructional support for staff as accountability for all students' achievement standards increase. Strategies, techniques, and methodology for coordinating a building focused on supporting all students, teachers, and parents in a changing educational system are outlined, with samples of practical tools. Test modifications, alternative grading, behavior plans for students as appropriate, parental rights, staff roles and responsibilities, and the role of building and district administrators in ensuring high expectations of success for all students in the building and district are discussed with choices for consideration in the decision-making process.

The Educator

Touch a life
Protect a life
Stretch a life
Shape a life
Propel a life
Wind it up one more time
Let it go
See it fly and flourish

Table of Contents

1

UNDERSTANDING THE SPECIAL EDUCATION MAZE

Maintaining schools of excellence as higher standards are implemented across the nation requires building principals to provide leadership to their staffs, by supporting team instruction, cooperative scheduling, and staff development activities for all grade levels and disciplines. As reported in the 15th Annual Report to Congress (1993), 94.4 percent of students receiving services in special education attend regular school. Of those students, 69.3 percent spend more than 40 percent of their school day in the general classroom (Ayers, 1994).

The 19th Annual Report to Congress (1997) indicated that the number of students who receive special education and the costs of those services continue to increase. During the 1995–1996 school year, 5.6 million children ages 3–21 received special education services. That is an increase of 3.5 percent compared to the 1994–1995 school year (Education Week, 14 January 1998).

Since 1975, federal and state regulations have required eligibility committees to determine appropriate services for students with disabilities by determining the existence of a disabling condition and an appropriate school program for each identified student. The committees must specify the amount and type of instruction in the least restrictive environment (LRE). The first consideration of the LRE is the regular classroom with supplemental services and support. The hierarchical continuum of services is then considered until the individual student's instructional needs are adequately met in the appropriate LRE.

Special education is a consuming concern for educators, parents, and students. Resource allocation and differing demands for fairness in the educational community from the perspective of staff and students are political issues that arise in school communities across the nation.

A tremendous knowledge base is required in order to understand the impact of situations that occur during the school day. Educational concerns that arise involve the appropriate delivery of special education services to students with disabilities and assessing its impact on others in an inclusive or mainstream setting. Another concern that arises is determining responsibilities of special education and regular-education teachers for grading, test modification, curriculum adaptation, instructional methodology modification, and discipline.

To help building-level administrators better understand the identified needs of disabled students and become participating members of the decision-making team, a review of eligibility determination is presented in this chapter. Although some states require that building administrators be involved in the eligibility meeting, many states do not, and the administrator present represents special education or pupil personnel.

THE ELIGIBILITY PROCESS

In order for administrators and teachers to understand students with special educational needs, it is imperative that stakeholders understand the process that identifies students as disabled, and how students with specific disabilities may react in class to teachers and peers in the classroom. One way to approach the identification process is to understand the legislation that regulates special education and the definitions of disabilities.

Congress approved the reauthorization of IDEA (Individuals with Disabilities Education Act) on June 4, 1997. The original legislation, Public Law 94-142, the Education for All Handicapped Children Act of 1975, was renamed the Individuals with Disabilities Education Act (IDEA) in 1990, and Congress reauthorized this bill in the 105th Congress.

Under federal regulations, there are 13 disabling conditions for school aged students that indicate an educational disability. Most states have adopted these disability categories in their state regulations, with some variations. (See Appendix A.)

The federally defined classifications (vary slightly state to state) enable eligibility committees to determine if an educationally-related disability exists for individual students. They include: autism, deaf-blindness, deafness, emotional disturbance, hearing impairment, mental retardation, multiple disability orthopedic impairment, other health impairments, specific learning disability, speech or language impairment, traumatic brain injury, and visual impairment.

Various states have developed regulations based on federal law, which dictate the procedural processes that local education agencies (school districts) must follow in determining if a child has an educational disability. These processes include the referral of students suspected of having a disabling condition, which involves parental notification of due process rights, parental permission for evaluation, a multidisciplinary psychoeducational evaluation, and determining eligibility. If a student is classified as disabled and eligible for services, the referral process then involves determining the disabling condition, appropriate services to be offered, and the location of services.

State regulations differ slightly, as education is a state, not federal responsibility. However, IDEA and other federal laws involving civil rights (such as the Americans with Disabilities Act, 1990, and Section 504 of the Rehabilitation Act, 1973) govern the guiding principles that each state must develop for determining the regulatory rules of special education compliance.

REFERRAL

When a student is having difficulty in school, a teacher has the ability to consult with a team of professionals in the school for suggestions on how to address a student's academic, social, or behavioral needs. In some states (for example, New Jersey, Maryland, and Virginia), a child study team (CST) is the building- level team, and prior to making a referral for special education services, this team must meet and discuss a child's needs. The CST develops suggestions for the teacher and those must be implemented. Following implementation, the teacher then reports to the CST on the results of the implemented suggestions. If the team suspects that a disabling condition exists, the CST recommends that a student be evaluated.

In states where CST are not mandated, districts often have building-level teams that serve a similar function. IDEA mandates that children have opportunities for remediation of academic, social, and behavioral issues prior to referral for special education. Referral forms must contain a section that indicates what strategies and modifications have been attempted to remediate the area of concern. A meeting between parents, teachers, psychologist, and administrator often takes place in order to communicate concerns and explain that a referral to the eligibility committee is recommended. Parents who agree to the referral give permission in writing to have their child evaluated by a multidisciplinary team.

TIMELINES

There are legal timelines that govern the referral, identification, and placement of eligible students for delivery of special education services. States vary in their interpretation of the federal regulations. In all cases, however, the following federal regulation applies: "Within 60 (school) days of the receipt of consent to conduct an initial evaluation of a student, the BOE shall arrange for appropriate special education services, as recommended by the eligibility committee" (IDEA, 1997).

Once a referral for an evaluation is completed, the building principal or chairperson of the eligibility committee[1] must be notified. If the referral is submitted to the principal, it is the responsibility of *the building principal* to ensure that the 5 day notification (to the chairperson) timeline is followed, as referrals are initiated at the *building level*.

This means that once a referral is made, parental permission is quickly obtained, the evaluation is completed and an eligibility meeting is held within 30 (school) days. The recommendation of the eligibility meeting is then sent to the Board of Education (BOE) for approval. Services must begin within 30

[1] The committee charged with determining the eligibility status of students with disabilities varies from state to state (CSE, ARD, IEP). Throughout this book, "eligibility committee" is used.

school days of the BOE approval. The purpose of the timeline is to ensure that students suspected of having a disabling condition are evaluated in an efficient manner and so that appropriate support and services can be provided in a timely fashion.

The role of the *building principal is significant throughout the referral process*. In many school districts, the building principal delegates the role in the prereferral process to the psychologist. However, it is important to note that state and federal regulations hold the *building principal* as the responsible party.

Quite often, building administrators, parents, and teachers want changes recommended by the referral and eligibility process to occur quickly. The intent of the stakeholders is positive, as people want children's needs to be met as soon as they are identified. However, the timeline works in favor of all stakeholders, including teachers, parents, and children. The due process rights for students and parents must be adhered to, for in the long run, they support the ability of school personnel to support students and their families throughout the children's educational careers. If questions or concerns are raised, parents have the opportunity—as do school personnel—to discuss concerns in a collaborative manner, resulting in a cooperative approach to helping a student achieve personal, family and school goals.

EVALUATION COMPONENTS

The multidisciplinary evaluation for an initial referral for a student suspected of having a disability includes, at minimum, psychological assessment of ability, academic achievement testing, a classroom observation, a social history, and a medical evaluation. Psychologists usually complete the ability (IQ) and projective assessments and classroom observations. Psychologists or special education teachers complete academic testing. School social workers usually complete the social histories. Classroom teacher(s) prepare reports to the committee of current classroom functioning and report card grades. In some states, educational evaluators complete the academic testing and observation, while psychologists complete those assessment components that only licensed, school psychologists may administer, such as ability testing (IQ), projectives, and behavioral analyses.

Students who are suspected of having motoric or speech-language disabilities require additional evaluation by speech-language therapists, occupational therapists, and/or physical therapists. For students with vision or hearing impairment, vision or hearing specialists conduct appropriate evaluations. If behavioral or attentional concerns exist, a screening tool to assess these areas might be administered, filled out by the teacher and parent, and scored by the psychologist. A referral to a medical provider might be the result of the behavioral/attention screen for further evaluation of neurological dysfunction or attention deficit, as these diagnoses are not made by school personnel, but by physicians. It is important to note that these medical evaluations are not at school expense, unless eligibility committees deem the additional assessments necessary in order to determine appropriate programs of services for students. Many times additional evaluations are requested by parents, but the results have no bearing on the determination of eligibility or services recommended for their children's educational program.

During the eligibility meeting, the various evaluations are reviewed. These include the social history, psychoeducational assessments, classroom observation, and teacher reports, and any other available data, which might include district-wide and classroom test results, discipline reports, and other information that can assist committees in understanding the educational concerns of children.

Assessments discussed are often a point of confusion for people attending the eligibility committee meetings or who read the assessment results. It is beneficial to all, especially the student, if faculty and administrators can read, interpret, and understand the results of the reports.

An appropriate role of the building administrator is to assist faculty in understanding test data. While a principal might refer people to the building psychologist or a special education teacher, a strong message is given to faculty if building administrators are knowledgeable about assessment components. If we want regular and special educators to work collaboratively in supporting *all* children, then administrators can reinforce collaborative concepts by having a sincere, basic understanding of how a teacher can read reports. The information presented in the rest of this chapter provides a resource from an assessment consumer's point of view. The purpose is to explain evaluative data that principals and teachers frequently see in eligibility documents, not to delineate every assessment detail.

PSYCHOEDUCATIONAL EVALUATIONS

The components of the psychoeducational evaluation include a psychological assessment, an individual achievement test (norm-referenced and/or criterion-referenced tests), a classroom observation, social history, and if needed, behavioral, motor skills tests, or language assessments.

The purpose of *norm-referenced* tests is for comparison with "expected" responses. These reference points provide the evaluator with the ability to identify the degree to which the answers of the student being assessed correspond to the responses of average peers of the same age or grade (Shapiro, 1996). When a suspected disabling condition is being investigated, a significant deviation from the average response is an important variable to consider. *Criterion-referenced* tests examine a student's mastery of specific skills, which are referenced to domains of behavior, rather than normative comparisons of age or grade peers (Shapiro, 1996). These indicators are helpful in determining strengths and weaknesses of students. They can also be helpful tools in combination with norm-referenced ability and achievement measures, when determining a child's eligibility as a disabled child.

PSYCHOLOGICAL ASSESSMENT

The evaluating psychologist administers an ability (IQ) assessment. The Wechsler Intelligence Scale for Children, Third Edition (WISC-III; 1991) is most commonly used for children ages 6–16 years. The Wechsler Adult Intelligence Scale (WAIS-R) for older adolescents (16 and older) and the Wechsler Preschool and Primary Scale of Intelligence—Revised (WPPSI-R) for young children (ages 4–6.5 years) are often used. The Stanford-Binet, Fourth Edition (Stanford-Binet IV) is also often used for students ages 2–23 years (Thorndike, Hagan, & Sattler, 1986). These tests measure the innate ability of children in various ways. The WISC-III results are reported in verbal and performance areas. There are subtests and results in each of these categories. The average scaled score for each subtest ranges from 8 to 12, with 10 being the average score. Variation, or scatter, within the verbal or performance areas or a discrepancy between the verbal and performance scores is often a point of discussion regarding a child's strengths and weaknesses and indicator of the possibility of a disability.

On the Stanford-Binet IV, subtests assess ability in the areas of general ability, verbal, quantitative and short-term memory skills, and reasoning skills in three areas. Again, the subtest scores are used to determine whether there are significant discrepancies within the tested areas or when compared to achievement tests.

Scores are reported in standard scores as intelligence quotients. A guide to the way commonly used WISC-III scores are reported can be found in Appendix B.

EDUCATIONAL EVALUATIONS

Psychoeducational evaluations are used to determine the levels at which students can perform on an individual measure of achievement. The following tests are typically used to evaluate a student's ability to achieve in the areas of reading, math, and written language at the appropriate grade or age level:

- Woodcock-Johnson Psychoeducational Battery-R (WJ-R; Woodcock and Johnson, 1989)
- Key Math-R (Connolly, 1988)
- Kindergarten and First Grade Readiness Test
- Gray-Oral Reading Tests-3 (GORT-3; Wiederholt and Bryant, 1992)
- Woodcock-Johnson Reading Mastery-R (WRMT-R; Woodcock, 1987)
- Test of Written Language-3 (TOWL; Hammill and Larsen, 1988)

Scores are reported as grade or age equivalent levels, percentiles and standard scores for each subtest and broad areas of math, reading, written language, and general knowledge are part of the normative data compiled. An example of frequently used WJ-R results can be found in Appendix C.

UNDERSTANDING TEST RESULTS

Test results are recorded in a variety of ways. Understanding the most common data school practitioners use is helpful, as teachers and administrators often meet with parents who are concerned about their child's educational program. It is important to recognize that standard scores (not grade equivalents) reflect a measure that enables evaluators to make valid comparisons between tests. This score forms a normative base of comparison, with the following ranges of value:

- Superior Range 130+
- High Average Range 116–129
- Above Average Range 111–115
- Average Range 90-110
- Low Average Range 85-89
- Below Average Range 75–84
- Deficient Range below 75

Standard scores reflect a typical measurement distribution, and offer a statistical basis for test analysis reflective of student ability and achievement.

If a student's intelligence quotient (IQ) is in the average to high average range and the achievement scores are below average, this is one example of a possible learning disability. A contrast between ability (IQ) and achievement is one measure of a discrepancy. However, a disability might or might not exist; it depends on the magnitude of the discrepancy.

If there is inter- (between) or intra- (within) test scatter, a 15-point discrepancy which indicates one standard deviation is a guide to a significant discrepancy. Because education involves many complex variables and an eligibility assessment involves many components, there is not an exact formula that is used to determine the classification of a learning disability. The general guide listed above affords the reader the opportunity to view a sample of how the evaluating psychologist looks at data in the eligibility process. The school psychologist, educational evaluator, and eligibility team members review the data collected to determine whether and how a child is eligible for services under state and federal regulations, based on how educational progress is affected.

GRADE EQUIVALENT SCORES

These scores are often misunderstood. When a testing instrument determines a grade equivalent for a child in a subtest area, it does not mean that a child is functioning at the grade level of students in the grade signified by the stated grade equivalent. It indicates that compared to other students in the student's grade, normed results indicate that the child was able to complete tasks at a higher or lower grade compared to same-grade peers, *not* students in the higher or lower grade.

For example, if a child is in fifth grade (5.6 GE) and scores at the 8.0 level, it does not mean that the student scored according to the way eighth graders would perform; rather the student scored in the eighth-grade range compared to fifth-grade peers. The score is an indicator that the child is performing well for his or her grade placement, but not necessarily performing at a level three years above the current grade. The standard score (not grade equivalent) should be used for comparison, for it is a statistical measure that can be compared among assessment devices. Professionals and parents often look at grade-equivalent scores as an indicator of growth. However, these tests were not created to be utilized in this manner. Relying on grade-equivalent scores creates and perpetuates confusion.

STANDARD SCORES

Standard scores are used when comparing data, because they are based on a curve of normal distribution (the Bell curve). If a child has a 98 standard score in math one year, and the next year has a standard score of 97, this does not indicate a lack of growth. If a standard score stays statistically the same (that is, within 10 points), it indicates that the child has shown progress, as measured against himself or herself. Tests are normed by age and grade, so if the standard score stays the same one year later, it means that the student's skill grew as expected for the *new* age and grade. If a standard score decreases significantly (close to one standard deviation—approximately 15 points), concern would be appropriate, because in this case the student would not have demonstrated growth in the tested area.

For example, if a child demonstrates a significant weakness in an achievement area (e.g., reading) and has a standard score of 74 in reading skills one year, and a 76 the next, this indicates that the child is demonstrating progress as compared to him- or herself. However, the child is not closing the gap compared to age peers. However, if this same child scored a 89 in the second year, the child would not only be showing individual gain, but the child would be demonstrating *progress* toward catching up to age peers; the gap between the standard score and the average (100) is smaller and statistically significant.

PERCENTILES

Reporting test results in terms of percentiles is a method of ranking scores against the normal distribution continuum (the Bell curve). Extreme scores are indicated at the top (99th percentile) and at the bottom (1st percentile). Few people score at these extremes. The 50th percentile indicates an average achievement (compared to 100 on an IQ test). Scores above the 75th percentile indicate a achievement in the top fourth. Scores below the 25th percentile show achievement in the bottom fourth as measured against age or grade peers.

STANINES

Stanine scores are based on an equal-interval measure—a relatively simple scale that assigns a single digit to a scale that indicates a ranking similar to percentiles. A stanine of 1 is assigned to those who score in the bottom four percent, while a stanine of 9 indicates people who score in the top four percent. Stanines of 2 or 8 are assigned to people who score the next 7 percentages counting from the bottom or the top. Stanines of 3 or 7 are given to people who score in the next 12 percentages. Stanines of 4 or

6 indicate scores in the next 17 percentages, and a stanine of 5 is given to people who score in the middle 20 percent.

ADDITIONAL PSYCHOLOGICAL EVALUATIONS

BEHAVIORAL AND PROJECTIVE ASSESSMENTS

There are instruments that assist members of the multidisciplinary team (school psychologist, educational diagnostician, and school social worker) in determining whether a child's emotional state is interfering with the ability to learn or demonstrate knowledge. Assessments commonly referred to in a behavioral assessment include the Conners' Rating Scales--Revised (CRS-R), School Social Behavior Scales (SSBS), Adaptive Behavior Inventory (ABI), Preschool and Kindergarten Behavior Scales (PKBS), Burks Behavior Rating Scale, Behavior Rating Profile (BRP-2), Disruptive Behavior Rating Scale (DBRS), Attention-Deficit/Hyperactivity Disorder Test (ADHDT, 1994), Freedom from Distractibility Index (subtests of the WISC-III). Most of these assessments involve checklists that parents and/or teachers complete, and that psychologists score. If a student is classified as an "emotionally disturbed" child, it is important to remember that this classification means that there is an emotional reason for a student's significant difficulty in school, as indicated by the classification. This does not indicate a medical or psychiatric condition of mental illness.

Although some students are classified as educationally emotionally disturbed by eligibility committees, only medical professionals may diagnose psychiatric disorders, prescribe medication, and identify attention deficit disorders. School assessments for attending to school tasks may indicate the need for medical evaluation, but *only physicians* can diagnose medical conditions.

ADAPTIVE BEHAVIOR SCALES

If the eligibility committee considers classifying a child as mentally retarded, an adaptive behavior scale is completed. This scale indicates the level of independence a child has by parental and/or teacher interview and observation in the following areas:

- Social skills
- Independence in self-help skills
- Daily living skills

The most commonly used tool is the Vineland Adaptive Behavior Scale (Sparrow, et. al, 1984). For younger students professionals use checklists such as the Brigance (Brigance Test of Early Development, 1980) or the Learning Accomplishment Profile--Diagnostic (LAP-D). These checklists give an age-equivalence for skills achieved in years and months, which can be compared to the chronological age of the child being evaluated.

PROJECTIVE ASSESSMENTS

Projective assessment tools are measures of emotional status that assist the psychologist in determiniing a child's emotional development. They are scored subjectively and are administered by trained psychologists in a school setting. These tests involve techniques used to analyze a student's feelings by what the student projects into a story, drawing, picture, or sentence completion (Overton, 1992). The analysis reveals needs, wants, desires, fears, and anxieties (Hopkins, 1998).

There are two types of projective tests commonly used in schools. These include drawing tests and sentence completion tests.

Drawing tests attempt to ascertain a student's feelings about self, family, and home life. Draw-a-Person (Machover, 1949) and House-Tree-Person (Buck, 1948), Thematic Apperception Test (Murray, 1943), are drawing tests frequently used. Students are asked to draw a self-portrait; a house, tree, and a person; or the family doing an activity together, respectively. Each aspect of the drawing is supposed to suggest psychological significance, including size, position, parts of the body, clothing, omission, etc. (Hopkins, 1998). The Draw-a-Person screening instrument is based on the child's self-portrait, and drawings of a man and a woman. This tool is based on a representative standardization sample, and reliability and validity data have been included.

Sentence completion tests ask students to finish partial sentences. The examiner analyzes the answers for themes, and follow-up questions elicit comments on issues involving relationships with parents and friends, and feelings. Two popular tests are the Rohde Sentence Completion Test (Rohde, 1957) and the Rotter Incomplete Sentences Blank (Rotter and Rafferty, 1950).

There are conflicting opinions on the value of these subjective tools, but they frequently provide information that is helpful in the evaluative process.

FINE MOTOR AND VISUAL PERCEPTION

In the area of fine motor or visual perception skills, a Developmental Test of Visual-Motor Integration, Third Edition (VMI-3; Beery, 1989), or a Bender Visual-Motor Gestalt Test (BVMGT; Bender, 1938) is often administered. These tests require that a student copy designs (simple to complex) of varying degrees of complexity. When a child has a learning disability, there often is a delay in the development of visual-motor integration. This may impact handwriting and reading. These two tests are examples of the tools psychologists or educational evaluators use to assess a student's strengths or weaknesses in fine motor skills and visual perception.

SOCIAL HISTORY

This required evaluative tool is completed by a school social worker, or another member of the multidisciplinary evaluation team. The parent is asked questions that give background information on the child, including birth history, medical history, and particular events that may have had an impact on the child's growth, as reported by the parent.

CLASSROOM OBSERVATION

A classroom observation is completed by the psychologist, social worker, or educational evaluator, as a mandated part of the evaluation. Recording a student's performance in the classroom can indicate differences from testing data. The observed behavior can also support presenting issues that impact the child in the classroom, which led to the referral.

MEDICAL EXAMINATION

The purpose of the medical examination is to rule out or identify any underlying physiological condition that might cause a student to present problems in school. For example, a student may have a medical condition (e.g., Tourette's syndrome, or some other specific neurological impairment) that causes certain behaviors in the classroom. This information would be very important to know when the eligibility team meets to discuss the evaluative results.

RELATED SERVICE EVALUATIONS AND PURPOSE

If a student with a disability is found eligible for special education services and is entitled to an individualized school program, additional support might be recommended by the eligibility committee through various disciplines as a related service. By federal mandate (IDEA 1997) related services are provided to support and assist a child in benefiting from special education.

Related services include transportation and such developmental, corrective, and other supportive services that are required to assist a child with a disability to benefit from special education (federal regulations, Sec. 300.22). The building administrator's role in facilitating the provision of related services is connected to the planning and implementation of the building schedule. Students with disabilities must be able to receive related services during an "elective" period, *not* during academic instruction from regular *or* special education class time. This can create conflicts in other school areas that must be balanced for the school, staff, and students.

If a child is suspected of having a motoric or speech-language impairment, the following related services therapists might be involved in evaluations prior to the eligibility meeting:

SPEECH AND LANGUAGE THERAPY

Typically, students who present with difficulty in articulation or the processing of expressive or receptive language will be evaluated by a speech therapist. The evaluator will use standardized tests (TOLD-R, CELF-R, Goldman-Fristoe Test of Articulation, OWL) to determine whether a disability in these areas exists, by comparing standard scores to a child's age- and ability- level peers.

OCCUPATIONAL AND PHYSICAL THERAPY

If a student has a motoric disability or significant muscular dysfunction related to mobility, safety, or the ability to participate in the school program, an occupational or physical therapy evaluation might be recommended.

OCCUPATIONAL THERAPY

Many parents and professionals believe that any difficulty with fine motor skills (cutting, drawing, puzzles, stringing beads) or handwriting (neatness, force) indicates a need for school-based occupational therapy (OT). This is *not* the case. OT in a school setting is provided to students who are classified as disabled and have an inability to coordinate small muscles in an age-appropriate manner that *adversely affects educational progress*. This disability can be demonstrated by significant weakness in fine motor or writing activities, but cannot be adequately addressed solely by classroom intervention.

Deficiencies in visual-spatial perception, self-help skills, and fine motor skills to a degree that meets the above criteria may require intervention by an occupational therapist. *Sensorimotor* and *perceptual* systems provide the core mechanisms by which people interact with the environment. The sensorimotor system involves receiving input to the sensory system from the environment and conducting an impulse into the nervous system with which a child processes information, which allow a child to notice and react to the stimuli. The perceptual system involves internal actions, which enable a child to interpret information that is utilized in cognitive, language, and motor tasks. Tests administered frequently for identifying sensorimotor and perceptual needs include the Bruininks-Oseretsky Test of Motor Development, the Peabody Motor Scale, Bender-Gestalt and the VMI.

Deficits in *sensory integration* (SI) qualify some students to receive occupational therapy in schools. An SI deficit is the inability to process input received through one of the five senses and coordinate sensory output. This can affect a child's ability to determine where his body is in space, cause significant adverse reactions to tactile stimulation, or cause a child to be in motor "overdrive," in which constant movement prevents a child from focusing. Messages received through the five senses send information to the brain, where the information is processed, and cause a response. Students with significant SI deficits receive the information, but the message gets jumbled along the nerve synapses, and the response is altered.

PHYSICAL THERAPY

Physical therapy (PT) in a school setting is provided to students who are classified as disabled, and have an inability to coordinate large muscles in an age-appropriate manner that *adversely affects educational progress*. The ability to navigate safely in the school environment is a primary indicator for school-based physical therapy.

Occupational and physical therapy consultation is often a service recommended, as the special education teacher can implement a program of fine and gross motor, visual-perceptual, and sensory or tactile activities as part of classroom activities. The therapist can assist the teacher with modifying activities in a manner that will enhance a child's motor development. For some children, the severity of need is minimal, and the classroom setting is the appropriate place to address the motor needs of a child. Only when the goals and objectives *cannot* be met appropriately within the classroom setting with the teacher, or consultative services by the therapist, is OT or PT provided for a child.

In most states in order for an occupational or physical therapist to evaluate and/or treat a child in the school setting, a physician must write a prescription. In a few states, OT may not require a prescription, but that condition is changing throughout the nation. Because both OT and PT are medically supported therapies, the professional organizations are recommending physician referrals for evaluation and treatment. However, there is a separation between medical and educational models of OT and PT, and the fact that a physician writes a prescription does not guarantee service. The therapist who evaluates the child will make the distinction of need for *educational purpose,* in accordance with federal and state regulations, and make recommendations to the eligibility committee.

THERAPY FOR STUDENTS WITH HEARING IMPAIRMENTS

Audiological services are provided for students with hearing loss. The determination of the nature and degree of hearing loss, and habilitative activities, such as sign language, cued speech, lip reading, total communication, and communication skills (receptive and/or expressive) might be provided as related services. Hearing aids or auditory trainers might also be provided as a related service.

THERAPY FOR STUDENTS WITH VISUAL IMPAIRMENTS

Students who are visually impaired receive assistance and habilitative activities as appropriate, which might include V-tek (enhanced vision technology) machines, computers, and Braille readers and typewriters. Orientation and mobility training might be provided to enable students to move safely within their schools, homes, and communities. Many school districts do not require a full-time teacher for hearing- or visually-impaired students, so qualified personnel provide itinerant services to students in a variety of school settings.

ASSISTIVE TECHNOLOGY

Assistive technologies support people with disabilities by providing direct assistance in the selection, acquisition, or use of assistive technology devices. This service includes evaluation, training, and technical assistance. It also includes providing, adapting, repairing, and coordinating the use of devices so the children can benefit from special education and related services.

Assistive technology encompasses many pieces of equipment. For students with significant writing disabilities, the use of word processors or computers with spelling and grammar checkers might be specified on IEP. For students with communication impairments, devices, such as a Dynovax system (a computerized, symbol and word-based communication device), that "speak" for nonverbal students might be specified on an IEP. Other students might need manual communication boards, visual readers (computer systems that translate text into spoken words), and textbooks on tape (usually through the National Library for the Blind).

Students who require assistive technology devices must be encouraged and allowed to use these tools throughout the school day, for homework, and for other school-related tasks. The building administrator must be aware of and assist staff in understanding its role in working with individual students and necessary equipment.

COUNSELING

The eligibility committee can recommend counseling for students who demonstrate the need for school-related counseling.

If a student is dealing with a pervasive issue that interferes with the ability to focus in school, this school-based support service might be recommended. For example, if a child is unable to make appropriate choices due to a disabling condition, is not attending classes, is not completing assigned tasks, or is getting involved in conflicts with other students in school, counseling might be suggested. If a student is functioning well in school, but is having difficulty at home with parental or family issues or problems within the community, counseling would not be recommended as a related service. Outside counseling to help deal with those issues might be suggested as a possible support mechanism for the student and the student's family.

ELIGIBILITY DETERMINATION

After all student evaluations are completed, the eligibility committee convenes. As part of due process rights for students, parents or guardians must receive written notification of the meeting at least five days prior to the scheduled meeting. School districts must have the meeting within the legal timeline, unless the parent requests that the meeting be rescheduled beyond that date.

Typically, the school psychologist and/or educational evaluator meet with the parents or guardians prior to the eligibility meeting to go over the results of the evaluations. Parents are informed of the recommendations that will be made to the eligibility committee, but the committee has the responsibility of determining whether a disabling condition exists, and what educational support is recommended for the child.

ELIGIBILITY MEETING

Parents are often intimidated by the eligibility meeting, for they walk into a room where numerous professionals with legal pads and reports are seated around a table. Parents need to be encouraged to participate, and to ask any questions they have. Parents and schools working collaboratively to foster a child's educational progress is the common goal.

MEMBERS OF THE ELIGIBILITY COMMITTEE

Federal guidelines mandate the skills and backgrounds of the members of the eligibility committee:

- The classroom teacher
- A special education teacher
- A person knowledgeable about available programs and services and about the general education curriculum (administrator)
- An evaluator
- One of child's parents or guardians.

One of the members must be able to understand evaluation results, otherwise an additional member is required who does understand such results (e.g., an educational evaluator, speech/language therapist, or a psychologist). In some states, the psychologist is also a mandated member of the committee. In some states a parent can require that a physician be a member of the committee provided that the parent make such a request at least 72 hours prior to the scheduled meeting. Some states have other mandated committee members, but the core requirements are the same.

At the eligibility meeting, results of the multidisciplinary evaluation are discussed, as well as data regarding the student's total school performance that are collected from current teachers (see forms in chapter 5 resource section), guidance counselors, and other school personnel. For some students, these data might include remedial support services, counseling, and disciplinary reports. Interventions attempted prior to the referral should also be discussed. Parents are often asked whether situations described by school personnel are similar to what they see at home, and parents have the ability to share information with the committee.

CLASSIFICATION

If a child is found eligible for services as a disabled student, services are recommended. The services should support academic, behavioral, social, and/or management needs of the student, based on individual needs. Consideration for the least restrictive environment (LRE) is determined at the eligibility meeting. The committee must first consider whether the student's needs can be met in the regular classroom or with supplemental support in the regular classroom. If not, then the continuum of LRE is considered in a hierarchical manner: supplementary pull-out services, part-time special education support, full-time special education support, full-time special classes in a private school setting, or residential placement. The LRE provision has been in place since the original P. L. 94-142 (1975). However, a federal audit of state programs during the late 1980s pointed out that most states were not focusing on the LRE clause. The audit found that too many students received services for more than 60 percent of the school day in segregated special education classes. After this audit, the federal government and locals schools refocused on LRE provision, which many educators believed to be a mandated inclusion movement in the early 1990s.

SERVICES AND IMPLEMENTATION OF THE INDIVIDUAL EDUCATIONAL PLAN

After a student is identified as educationally disabled, the eligibility committee develops an individual education plan (IEP). This plan identifies the student's disabling condition, and describes basic information about the student in physical, social-emotional, behavioral, and educational areas. Strengths and weakness of the child are identified, and goals and objectives are developed to guide the annual school plan for the child's educational program for subjects and areas identified by the eligibility team.

An IEP must include the following elements:

- A disability classification
- A placement recommendation
- The date of implementation
- A triennial review date
- A projected annual review date

The IEP must also include a statement regarding the frequency, location, and duration of special education and related services. It must outline mainstreaming opportunities. Furthermore, the plan must include an LRE statement that delineates the *reasons why and the extent, if any, to which the child will* ***not*** *participate with nondisabled peers in the regular class and in other activities*. The IEP must also include delineation of appropriate test modifications and descriptions of any specialized equipment or adaptive devices needed for the student to benefit from education. Measurable annual goals that are consistent with a student's needs and abilities, short-term instructional objectives, and evaluation criteria and methodology for measuring progress toward stated goals and objectives must be described. A statement of how the student's parents or guardians will be regularly informed of their child's progress toward annual goals and the extent to which that progress is sufficient to enable the student to reach the goals by the end of the year must be at least as often as parents are informed of their nondisabled peers' progress (i.e., the report card schedule).

For students age 14 and older, a statement of transition services needed and interagency linkages must be a component of the IEP. Post high school activities (such as work, college, and job training) are considerations for students and data are gathered through vocational assessments, guidance plans, and parental and student surveys.

The eligibility committee must address the unique needs of the child that arise from his or her disability in order for the child to progress in the *general education curriculum*. The House Committee Report (IDEA, 1997)emphasized that the majority of children identified as eligible for special education and related services are capable of participating in the general education curriculum to varying degrees with necessary adaptations and modifications.

An IEP is *not* a daily lesson plan. Rather the IEP should reflect the proposed program of *annual* goals and objectives that enable the child to be involved and progress in the general curriculum, and evaluative criteria reported as an indication of how the objectives will be met. The IEP reflects curricular goals and individual student needs, indicating how an individual child can meet curricular standards of proficiency.

In some states (e.g., New Jersey, Maryland, and Virginia) the IEP is signed by the committee participants and the parents or guardians. In other states (i.e., New York and Pennsylvania) signatures are not required on the IEP. However, the parents of the student with a disability must sign permission for the recommended services and placement. The board of education then approves the eligibility determination and the services are implemented in accordance with the IEP.

COMMON TERMS

TESTING TERMS

Achievement test—measures academic skills; identifies strengths and weaknesses in academic and developmental areas.

AE—age equivalence.

Chronological age—actual age of child.

Eye-hand coordination—skills that coordinate what is seen with what hands do, such as puzzle completion, coloring in lines, and cutting.

Fine motor skills—abilities that involve the use of small muscles in hands and wrists that allow for planful coordination with activities such as drawing, writing, cutting, pasting, completing puzzles, and stringing beads.

GE—grade equivalence.

IQ—intelligence quotient, which indicates a child's innate ability.

Standard score—a statistically accepted measure used to compare between tests and test items.

Visual perception—the ability to process visual stimuli, including remembering and retaining what is seen (Overton, 1992).

LEGAL TERMS

Amendment—minor change to the IEP through committee process.

Annual review—the yearly review of a student's IEP to determine subsequent programs and services.

Eligibility committee—a multidisciplinary evaluation team that meets to determine whether a student presents with a disabling condition. The committee determines the specific disabling condition, and determines appropriate programs and services, and the location where services will be provided.

IEP—individual education plan.

IEP team—in some states (e.g., Oregon, Virginia, and Maryland) this group is the same as the subcommittee.

Initial review—the first time a student is evaluated to determine whether an educational disabling condition exists.

LRE—least restrictive environment.

Special Review—a review of programs or services prior or in addition to the annual review.

Subcommittee—a team that convenes to review a disabled student's program and progress. (See *IEP team* above.)

COMMON ABBREVIATIONS FOR CLASSIFICATIONS

ADD/ADHD—attention deficit disorder/attention deficit hyperactivity disorder.

ED—emotionally disturbed/disabled.

LD—learning disabled.

MR—mentally retarded.

NI—neurologically impaired.

SI—speech impaired.

TBI—traumatic brain injury.

VI—visually impaired.

RELATED SERVICES

CO—counseling.

OT—occupational therapy.

PT—physical therapy.

ST—speech therapy.

TEST MODIFICATIONS/GRADING

If a student's IEP specifies alternative testing and test modifications, *all teachers* who work with the child must abide by the modifications indicated on the IEP. Testing situations can be altered and testing methods can be modified according to the following examples.

- Extending time allocated for tests
- Testing the student in a separate location from other students being tested
- Recording answers to test questions

- Excusing a student's spelling or grammatical errors
- Reading questions to the student
- Providing tests in alternative formats (e.g., with no essay questions, or as multiple choice only).

The eligibility committee determines test modifications on an individual basis, based on a student's disability.

The purpose of test modifications is to equalize the testing situation due to the nature and severity of a child's educational disability. Test modifications enable students with disabilities to participate in test programs on an equal basis with peers (Viola, 1995). Frequently, educators complain that students entitled to test modifications have an unfair advantage over non-disabled peers. In determining a student's need for modifications, emphasis should be placed on the necessity for modification, not "merely the potential benefit from modification" (SED, 1995). Test modifications are intended to allow students to demonstrate knowledge. They provide access and the ability for students with disabilities to demonstrate achievement and knowledge, with appropriate modifications based on the nature and severity of their disabilities. For example, no one would ask a blind child to read a test without a Braille reader, or ask a deaf student to listen to a passage without an interpreter or a written passage. However, appropriate modifications for learning disabled or emotionally disabled students are less apparent, and teachers perceive modifications provided as an unfair advantage for students who "don't really need them," or "take advantage of the system." This is not the case, for the eligibility committee determines the appropriateness of test modifications, not students or individual teachers.

It is important to remember that testing tools are used for different purposes. The individual achievement measures used as part of the eligibility determination provides data about the individual child in a one-on-one testing situation. Group testing with peers provides an opportunity for children to participate in what everyone else in the class or grade is doing; it gives an idea of how a child can perform in a group testing situation compared to individual achievement and ability; and it allows a child to be part of a typical school activity. In chapter 3, strategies for utilizing alternative methods enabling students to demonstrate knowledge are discussed.

Educators are beginning to focus on brain research. Jensen (1998) delineated the significant relationship between the importance of acknowledging how students at various stages of development best learn and demonstrate knowledge. Practitioners use many of the strategies he identified. Often, however, educators do not understand how the concepts of cooperative learning, peer tutoring, multisensory instructional techniques connect to a student's ability to learn and process information. Jensen (1998) identified the importance of setting goals, providing a positive learning environment, eliminating threat by adding transition time for students, increasing feedback and activating the emotional strength of students in the classroom. These concepts are consistent with the four major areas of an IEP: academic, physical, social/emotional and behavioral. Although educators had understood why these areas of development should be considered and addressed, the significance of how they relate to the function of the brain was not well understood.

Other educators and researchers (Dunn, 1996; Gardner, 1993; Marzano, 1992) compiled information regarding how students learn differently from one another based upon individual interests and strengths. They also focused on how teachers can provide opportunities that enable students to demonstrate knowledge in different ways. In chapters 3 and 4, there are suggested staff development activities that building leaders can introduce and lesson plan options that classroom teachers can implement. Both integrate theories of brain research into practice.

TEST EXEMPTIONS

The eligibility committee can exempt a child from taking state tests, but with new graduation standards in many states, this exemption would negate the opportunity for the child to earn a typical high school diploma. A better alternative for most students is to have the appropriate test modifications which would enable the child to demonstrate knowledge in an appropriate manner.

Children who are severely disabled and cannot be expected to take competency exams should not participate in state or district testing programs. In such cases, the IEP should reflect test-exempt status so that children do not need to attempt inappropriate state or district exams.

ANNUAL REVIEWS

At least once a year, each child's IEP *must* be reviewed by the eligibility committee or subcommittee in order to determine the continued appropriateness of the special education program and make adjustments as necessary. Meetings may be scheduled at any time throughout the year by parents or teachers in order to make adjustments to the IEP.

Changes in program or services require an eligibility committee meeting in order to comply with regulations. Changes to program or services can only be made through this process before any adjustments are made to a student's programs or services:

1. The eligibility committee reviews the IEP and student's status and progress.
2. The eligibility committee makes recommendations for any changes and forwards its recommendations to the board of education.
3. Once the board of education approves the recommendations, changes can then be implemented.

Annual reviews can be held throughout the school year. Many districts plan annual reviews on the anniversary of students' entrances into special education programs. Other districts schedule meetings during the second semester. Although it might seem illogical to plan early in a school year for the following school year, it is important to note that schools often plan student schedules—especially at the secondary level—by January of each school year.

School districts schedule eligibility meetings 12 months a year. Students who are not in special education need schedule changes due to failing classes, summer school credit, switching electives, and students in special education have similar reasons for schedule changes. In addition, special education program and/or related services might need to change, necessitating an eligibility meeting.

However, for most students, especially those at the elementary level, recommendations for special education program and services can be projected accurately. Secondary-school annual review meetings should correspond to district planning for secondary scheduling, as typical changes occur for all students throughout the spring and summer.

2

Laws Governing Special Education in Public Schools

Special education in public schools has generated significant legal debate in the United States for decades. Congress passed laws to ensure a "free, appropriate education (FAPE) for all children," and these laws have created a litigious world in which the term "appropriate" has been redefined by federal courts. Between the mid-1980s and 1997, parents and attorneys challenged placements, not because public schools did not provide a free and appropriate education, but because due-process challenges bypassed state hearings and these challenges were moved by family lawyers into the federal courts. Judges in the federal court system were not educators and trained litigators presented cases that appeared to show that educators were not assisting students adequately. Educators who were called as witnesses were intimidated by lawyers familiar with trying cases in federal court, and implied that intimidated teachers were poor teachers; lawyers claimed teachers were not teaching disabled children appropriately. When judges were asked to send students to private school as a way of assuring appropriate education for disabled students, many times school districts settled rather than tie up administrators and teachers in a lengthy, disturbing process. Judges ruled in some cases that a private school "couldn't hurt," rather than address the appropriateness of a placement.

Understandably, non-educators have and had difficulty interpreting the special education maze. It sounds reasonable that if a child is not progressing at a desired rate, something different in schooling should occur. However, what is not well understood by professionals unfamiliar with special education is that the nature and severity of some students' disabilities negate the issues raised as the reasons for district-sponsored, private-school placement. Private schools often demonstrate no additional progress with students and have no accountability within federal special education regulations. Private schools can choose their students and are not held to FAPE requirements.

Beginning in 1996, public school districts began challenging federal-court decisions by fighting and winning cases at the appellate level. In 1997 and 1998, cases in the Second, Fourth, Eighth, and Twelfth circuits were decided in favor of school districts. The circuit court judges chastised lower courts for being "out of sync" with Congressional laws and federal regulations. FAPE was reinforced as the standard to use in placement disputes. Judgments issued harsh reprimands to lower court judges, reminding them that Congress never intended to take educational decisions away from the educators (Hartmann, 1997).

The IDEA (1997), ADA, (1990) and Section 504 of the Rehabilitation Act (1973), moreover, contained protections that apply to students with disabilities. These acts state that *all* educators need to be aware of and helpful in implementing free and appropriate educations for students with disabilities. Special education administrators and building and central office administrators need to assist one another in the challenge of supporting *all* students in achieving educational goals. Further, as educators, we need to increase our shared knowledge to reach team and organizational goals.

LEGAL COMPLIANCE

One of the most difficult issues for educational leaders in school organizations to understand is the significant body of law that surrounds special education compliance. Many people perceive regulations as complex, cumbersome, and at times, unfair. The amount of paperwork required throughout the eligibility and IEP process can seem overwhelming. However, the legal structure provides a framework of support. Even though some stakeholders might not agree with the regulations, compliance *is mandatory*.

In a typical school setting, special education is often left to the special education teachers and special education administration. Assumptions abound that "they" will take care of things. The realization that "they" are "we" must occur, because most children who receive special education services also spend a percentage of their day in regular classrooms. In fact, IDEA (1997) focuses on higher standards and expectations, including increased time in regular classrooms for students with disabilities, general education curriculum for all students, and *shared accountability* for student outcomes. Educators need to join together and work collaboratively on behalf of all students.

Building and central office leaders must *share* this responsibility as well. Directors of special education or pupil personnel services need building-level and district administrators to understand their supportive roles. Knowledge *is* the key along with the guidance and assistance of district administration that is responsible for special education services and programs.

IDEA Concepts

Entitlements under IDEA

One of the toughest challenges for schools is explaining IDEA special education entitlements to various constituencies. Parents want the best for their children; boards of education want to ensure fiscal responsibility by central office administrators; directors of special education and pupil personnel services—as chairpersons of the eligibility process—are given the task of ensuring that appropriate services, programs, and related services are provided to students with disabilities. Teachers ask for increased services *outside* of the regular class setting to assist students. Parents ask for additional support *in* the classroom for their children. Confusion regarding entitlements ensues. Legal challenges occur, further challenging entitlements, wants, and needs.

A misunderstood premise is that "more is better" or that "optimal" program support is a requirement or entitlement. Two recent court cases at the federal appellate level supported public schools in the clarification of disabled student entitlements.

In July 1997, the U.S. Court of Appeals, Fourth Circuit, rendered a decision in *Hartmann v. Loudoun County*. The case involved a student and his family regarding the inclusion issue, which is discussed later in this chapter. However, statements in court decisions are germane to the discussion of entitlements under IDEA. They include:

- IDEA does not "guarantee the ideal educational opportunity for every disabled child."
- States must provide specialized instruction and related services "sufficient to confer some educational benefit upon the handicapped child, but the Act does not require the furnishing of every special service necessary to maximize each handicapped child's potential."

In April, 1998, the U.S. Court of Appeals, 2nd Circuit, decided a case (*Walczak V. Florida Union Free School District* (97-7155)), and stated that a public school district did not have to pay for a student's private school education, because she was making adequate progress in her current public school program. In the decision, the Court said that:

- The student's academic progress satisfied the IDEA showing that the school had succeeded in providing an appropriate, free, public education.
- "IDEA does not require states to develop IEPs that maximize the potential of handicapped children," citing the U.S. Supreme Court's 1982 decision in *Board of Education v. Rowley* (458 U.S. 176).

In many circumstances, parental and teacher requests exceed entitlements. Denials of requests are difficult for caring individuals to understand, when all involved are focused on perceived needs of the disabled child. *Entitlement issues* frequently arise throughout the country over the provision of related services, tutoring, location of services (home vs. school), and summer school classes.

Clarifying these issues in accordance with state regulations and federal laws is crucial for understanding. By regulation, related and support services are provided to school-age students in individual or group settings, a minimum of once or twice a week. For severely impaired students, related services may be provided up to five times a week. These services are school-based entitlements. Parental requests for services in the evening or over the weekend are not student entitlements as schools offer services during the school day. A parent has the right to refuse services during the day and to arrange for private services during non-school hours, but the district does not pay for these services. The IEP might stipulate that related services be available to the child during the school day, but parents can choose alternatives at their expense. For example, a request for the provision of therapy at home as a related service is *not* an entitlement.

Resource-room or skill-support classes offered to students during the school day cannot be replaced by after-school tutoring by parental request, for such services are not entitlements under IDEA. Although there might be *exceptions* when unique situations arise, they are decided on an individual basis by the eligibility committee.

Another area of continual confusion pertains to the entitlement of year-round special services or programs. Federal (300.5) and state regulations specify who is eligible for 12-month services:

- Students whose management needs are determined to be highly intensive and require a high degree of intervention
- Students with severe, multiple disabilities, whose programs consist primarily of habilitation
- Students who, because of their disabilities, need a program in order to *prevent substantial regression* as determined by the eligibility committee.

A student experiences *substantial regression* when disabilities prohibit the child from regaining skills within a reasonable time after the start of a new school year (within a few months). Students who receive services in a 10-month school program typically are ineligible for 12-month services, although some students require summer services based on the above criteria.

Schools frequently offer summer-school programs for students. It is *illegal* to exclude categorically students with disabilities from these summer-school programs. The criteria for student participation must be applied to all students, *except* those with disabilities who are entitled to 12-month services. Entitlements to testing modification, as delineated in the IEP, *do* continue for summer-school classes and assessments, for the student's disability does not go on summer vacation.

LEAST RESTRICTIVE ENVIRONMENT

Students identified as being educationally disabled are entitled by law to receive services in the least restrictive environment, as appropriate. The first consideration is supplemental support provided in the regular classroom, which offers the least restrictive environment. For some students, this level and location of service is appropriate. For other students, more restrictive settings offer the least restrictive environment. The full LRE continuum of services is appropriate for individual students; students' disabilities and learning styles determine the most appropriate LRE.

A child has the right, and the eligibility committee the responsibility, of trying the least restrictive environment before determining that a placement is inappropriate for a student. It might be determined that the first environment tried is inappropriate for a child and the child needs to move to a more restrictive environment, which would then be the LRE for the child.

If a child is going through initial eligibility consideration and a parent requests part-time special education services to see whether the child will progress, and if no safety issues are present, the eligibility committee has to determine which option on the continuum of services represents the LRE and whether a less restrictive setting should be attempted. It would be difficult to "jump" down the continuum without attempting part-time services in this situation. The eligibility committee might schedule another meeting after a specified period in order to determine whether a more restrictive setting is indicated.

INCLUSION AND THE LEAST RESTRICTIVE ENVIRONMENT

School administrators across the country have expressed concern about inclusive practices. They are concerned about complying with the LRE requirements of the IDEA, and they want to ensure that a full continuum of services exists for children who are eligible for services as students with a disability. Building principals are concerned about how to manage the schedules of teachers, students, and program components within budgetary constraints. Class size is growing, resources are limited, and the management of an ever-changing, diverse student body demands attention.

Between 1989 and 1992, the federal government audited many state programs for disabled students, including Maryland, Florida, and New York. Of the 165 districts that were monitored, 143 districts failed to place disabled students in the least restrictive environment with non-disabled peers, as required by the IDEA (Special Education Report, March 1993). State departments of education were told to review these practices, and create policies that would be consistent with federal regulations. These revised policies have increased the number of inclusive classes. Furthermore, many students receive special education services in regular classrooms for part of the school day. Providing staff support for team-teaching in inclusive settings is a significant issue for building administrators. Offering strategies to teachers for instructing all students in a shared teaching environment is a staff-development need for all teachers and administrators. Administrators' understanding of how inclusion can help provide shared resources for student instruction will support all members of the school community.

The implementation of inclusive programs in the early 1990s were perceived to be poorly planned and executed in schools, leaving teachers, administrators, and parents confused and concerned about educating disabled and non-disabled students. The Americans with Disabilities Act (1990) and IDEA (1990) created an awareness of the educational rights of disabled children. Although educators, lawyers, and the media interpreted these laws as mandates for inclusion, in fact Public Law 94-142, the Education for All Handicapped Children Act of 1975, mandated that all children were entitled to a "free, public education," in the least restrictive environment." Once a child was determined to be eligible for services as a disabled child, the law required that services and the location of those services be based on individual needs. A regular classroom setting with support was the first setting in which providing services was considered, because the classroom is the least restrictive environment. If the regular classroom with support cannot adequately meet the child's educational needs, only then can a more restrictive setting be considered in which to deliver special education services to a student.

These regulations were interpreted by some school districts to mean that all children, regardless of severity of disability, be educated in the regular classroom, in their neighborhood school. Unfortunately, some school districts in many states decided to assign all students, regardless of disability, to regular classes, guided by boards of education, superintendents, parent groups, and other perceived political influences. The rapid response of these districts showed that changes in special education service delivery can occur overnight. In situations thus described, central administration believed that this changeover would help students and ensure that their school systems would comply with new regulations and prevent legal challenges. In reality, this immediate change created resentment, anger, and confusion for all participants. The philosophical change resulted in a chaotic educational environment for the students that the systemic change was supposed to help.

There have been many legal challenges involving inclusion. In 1982, the U.S. Supreme Court heard the *Board of Education of Hendrick Hudson Central School District v. Rowley*. The court's decision supported that the district recommendation for placement of a disabled child was appropriate because the district had "reasonably calculated to enable the child to receive educational benefits." The court stated that the Education for All Handicapped Children Act (1975) does not require states to realize to the greatest degree the potential of each disabled child (Aefsky, 1995).

Between the 1980s and mid 1990s, legal decisions involving inclusion supported services for children to be provided in the regular classroom (Oberti, 1992; Holland, 1994), if the nature and severity of the disabilities warranted the regular classroom settings as the LRE. The courts determined a six-facet test to determine LRE through these cases. Decisions were also made that supported schools that segregated children (Daniel, R., 1989; DeVries, 1989; Hartmann, 1997), when appropriate.

The *legal standards* for determining whether a recommended placement represents the least restrictive environment include the following:

- Ability of the child to achieve the IEP goals within the regular education program with the assistance of supplementary aids and services.
- Evidence that the board of education has made efforts to modify the regular educational program to accommodate a child with disabilities.
- Consideration of the unique benefits—academic or otherwise—that the child might receive by remaining in the regular class.
- The fact that a child might make greater *academic* progress in a segregated classroom may not warrant excluding a child from the regular classroom.
- Consideration of the negative effects of inclusion on other children. (This includes an inquiry of whether a functional behavior plan was implemented for the child in the LRE.)

Many legal challenges were won by proponents of inclusion. These judgments favorable to inclusion were due to the fact that the LRE provisions of the law were not understood to be an *entitlement* of students with disabilities. Students were offered services in segregated settings; administrators did not consider placing learning disabled children in the regular classroom first. As stated earlier, this does not mean that every disabled child must be placed in a regular classroom before receiving services in a segregated location. It **does** mean, however, that eligibility committees must consider the regular classroom and that for some students, providing supplemental support in the regular classroom for services is appropriate.

In 1997, the U.S. Court of Appeals, Fourth Circuit, heard *Hartmann v. Loudoun County*. In this case parents of an elementary-school child appealed a lower court ruling that *did not support* inclusion for their child. The school district (approximately 45 miles west of Washington, DC) had provided an inclusive setting for Mark Hartmann, who entered the district as a first grader, formerly of Illinois. During his kindergarten year in Chicago, he had been placed in an inclusive setting, which was continued in Loudoun County, Virginia. Mark was very disruptive (screaming, hitting, and kicking) to the learning environment, even though classmates were hand-picked, class size was smaller than others in the grade and school, and an aide was with Mark full-time. The school district recommended a special education class in another school that Mark could attend and get support he needed to progress educationally and socially. He had the opportunity for mainstreaming in that school, but would receive primary education in a smaller, structured special education class.

His parents refused the placement, and the school district initiated a due process hearing. The district won the hearing, and the parents went to federal court, where they won. The district then appealed the decision in federal appellate court (Fourth circuit) and won. The U.S. Supreme Court refused to hear the case, allowing the appeals ruling to stand. The excerpts included below are taken from the decision of the appellate court in this ruling:

- IDEA "embodies important principles governing the relationship between local school authorities and a reviewing district court." Although, the law provides district courts with the authority to grant "appropriate" relief based on a preponderance of evidence, it is by no means an invitation to the courts to substitute their own notions of sound educational policy for those of the school authorities which they review.
- The "task of education belongs to the educators who have been charged by society with that critical task."
- These "principles reflect the IDEA's recognition that federal courts cannot run local schools."
- Local educators "deserve latitude in determining the individualized education program most appropriate for a disabled child."
- IDEA "does not deprive these educators of their right to apply their professional judgment."
- IDEA's mainstreaming provision establishes a presumption, *not* an "inflexible federal mandate." Dis-

abled children are to be educated with non-disabled children only to the "maximum extent appropriate." It explicitly states that "mainstreaming is not appropriate when the nature and severity of the disability is such that education in regular classes with the use of supplementary aids and services cannot be achieved satisfactorily."

The following excerpts show the federal court admonishing the lower court regarding its decision:

- Dismissing Loudoun County teachers' qualifications is to "adopt exactly the sort of potential-maximizing standard rejected by the Supreme Court in *Rowley*."
- IDEA does not require special education service providers to have "every conceivable credential relevant to every child's disability."
- Mainstreaming is inappropriate when "the handicapped child is a disruptive force in the non-segregated setting."
- The lower court "failed to mention, let alone discuss, critical administrative findings inconsistent with its conclusions. While making much of the credentials and witnesses endorsing full inclusion, the court gave little or no attention to the testimony of Loudoun professionals."
- IDEA encourages mainstreaming, but only to the "extent that it does not prevent a child from receiving educational benefit."
- Loudoun County "properly proposed to place Mark in a partially mainstreamed program which would have addressed the academic deficiencies of this full inclusion program while permitting him to interact with non-handicapped students to the greatest extent possible."
- This professional judgment by local educators was "deserving of respect."

This decision supported public educators more strongly than any legal decision to date. The statements of the justices on the Court of Appeals to the lower court judges indicated frustration that other court decisions, including *Rowley* and *DeVries*, were seemingly ignored. The fact that the Supreme Court refused to hear this case indicates that the results of the *Holland* and *Rowley* decisions are the "law of the land."

Federal appellate cases have continued to uphold the concept that judges are not trained educators and therefore, "judicial review under IDEA is limited" (US Court of Appeals for the Eighth Circuit, No. 196, 1998). The Supreme Court refused to hear an appeal in *Hartmann v. Loudoun County*, leaving intact the ruling by the U.S. Fourth Circuit Court of Appeals. They cited *Rowley* and the determination that IDEA does not require that every special service be furnished to maximize each disabled child's potential. The court further applied this concept to teacher qualifications. Teachers licensed and certified by the state need not have expertise in every conceivable disability. The Supreme Court also refused to hear a Fifth Circuit Court case (*Michael F. v. Cypress-Fairbanks Independent School District*; 97-691), in which it was determined that the school district had provided an appropriate education. Parents had requested payment for a residential school placement. Not only did the court support the school district placement, but also ordered the parents to reimburse the district for court costs.

SECTION 504

Section 504, part of the Rehabilitation Act of 1973, prohibits discrimination against people—including those with disabilities—in school systems that receive federal funds. Complying with Section 504 is *not* the responsibility of special educators; complying with Section 504 is the responsibility of the building administrator. All children who receive services under IDEA are automatically eligible for entitlements under Section 504. However, there are students who are not eligible under IDEA and are eligible for 504 plans.

In order for a child to be covered under 504, there must be a "physical or mental impairment which substantially limits a major life activity" (e.g., walking, seeing, hearing, speaking, breathing, learning, working, caring for oneself, and performing manual tasks). Section 504 requires from schools the following for eligible children:

- ♦ **An evaluation** by a group knowledgeable of the student and his or her disabilities using information from a variety of sources to determine the existence of a disability and its effect on one major life activity—learning.
- ♦ **A written plan** that details reasonable accommodations that ensure physical or instructional modifications are made to the regular education program.
- ♦ **Procedural safeguards** provided under Section 504 guarantee parents the right to proper notice, the right to participate in the student identification process, and the right to be represented by counsel. (The rights are less stringent, however, than those required under IDEA.)

Parents can appeal to the Office of Civil Rights or seek court intervention if they disagree with school recommendations, but they are encouraged to use grievance procedures established in the school district as a first step. Districts in violation of Section 504 can lose federal funding. Teachers who do not provide specified classroom modifications can be sued individually if the district Section 504 plan is not followed.

DISCIPLINE

Discipline related to students with disabilities can create conflict for building administrators. Since the U.S. Supreme Court decision in *Honig v. Doe* (1988), discipline involving students with disabilities has been confusing and misconstrued. Some administrators believe classified students cannot be disciplined in any way. Others believe all students, regardless of classification, should receive typical consequences of actions resulting from referrals.

In 1988, the Supreme Court decision in *Honig* reinforced the following provisions of the Education for All Handicapped Children Act (1975): All students, including those with serious emotional disturbances, are entitled to a comprehensive system of procedural safeguards that are designed to encourage meaningful parental participation in all aspects of a child's educational placement; the opportunity for an impartial due-process hearing with respect to any complaints parents have concerning placement; and the right to seek administrative review of any decisions they think inappropriate. The "stay-put" provision of the act directs that "a disabled child shall remain in his/her then current educational placement" pending completion of the review proceedings, unless the parents and local school district otherwise agree.

In *Honig v. Doe,* two students who were classified as emotionally disturbed were suspended indefinitely for violent and disruptive conduct related to their disabilities, pending expulsion proceedings by the San Francisco Unified School District. In the *Honig v. Doe* decision, Supreme Court Justice William Brennan delivered the opinion of the Court (emphasis added):

- "[P]ending completion of EHA proceedings, a school district *cannot take disciplinary action other than a 2- or 5-day suspension* against *any disability-related misconduct,* effecting a change in the educational placement of the child *without parental consent* pending procedural outcomes . . . ."
- [A]n indefinite suspension in aid of expulsion constitutes a change in placement under EHA . . . ."
- Congress did not leave school administrators powerless to deal with dangerous students, as *temporary suspensions of up to 10 school days for students posing an immediate threat to others' safety are allowed* under the EHA . . . ."
- [I]n those cases in which *parents* of a truly dangerous child adamantly *refuse to permit any change* in placement, the 10-day respite gives school officials an opportunity to invoke the aid of the courts, which have the right to grant injunctive relief if a student is sub-

stantially likely to result in injury either to him/herself or others . . . ."

Under IDEA reauthorization (1997), disciplinary procedures for students with disabilities were extended to include some nonclassified students. Such students must meet one or more of the following criteria:

- The student's parents have expressed in writing that they feel their student needs special education.
- The student's parents have requested an evaluation for special education services.
- The student's behavior or performance demonstrates a need for special education.
- The student's performance or behavior in school has caused concern among school personnel.

Students who are eligible for services or students who are in one of the categories listed above can be suspended for a total of 10 school days in a single school year. The total is cumulative and includes in-school and out-of-school suspensions. If the student is suspended for more than 10 days in a school year, that is tantamount to changing placement and according to the law parents must be notified immediately. There also must be an IEP/eligibility meeting to accomplish the following:

- Determine whether the conduct is a manifestation of the student's disabling condition
- Decide which services can be made available to address the behavior (e.g., counseling)
- Agree to a functional behavior intervention plan as part of the IEP (see sample p. 55)

For any other action, a student with a disability or a nonclassified student who meets the above criteria, the IEP/eligibility committee must determine whether there is a causal relationship between the disabling condition and the action. If there is no causal relationship, the building administrator can proceed with regular education disciplinary proceedings. However, parents must be notified of the results of the committee's manifestation determination and the school must follow due-process and procedural safeguards. Parents have the right to challenge decision and the right to challenge placement.

If a causal relationship between the student's behavior and the disability exists, then disciplinary options include the following:

- Reviewing and adjusting the IEP
- Suspending the student less than 10 days
- Placing the student in an IAES with parental consent

Suspensions of less than 10 cumulative days (compiled over the course of the school year) are under the building administrator's control. Suspensions must be consistent to the extent applicable with nondisabled students. However, it is significantly important to note that **any** suspension of a disabled student could result in a due-process challenge. Therefore, it would be to the benefit of the principal, superintendent, board of education, and organization to consult with the eligibility chairperson to ensure that regulations are being followed. This does not mean that the building administrator cannot suspend a child, but should coordinate district and state regulatory requirements. If the actions of a student initiate a suspension and the number of days suspended are approaching the cumulative 10-day benchmark, the eligibility committee should meet and determine whether or not the action (behavior) was due to the nature and severity of a student's disabling condition. This enables the eligibility committee to meet prior to the regulatory requirement. If a student's action will place him or her over the 10 day limit, the child may have to attend school until the eligibility meeting, unless parents agree to keep the student home. It is preferable to schedule a meeting prior to this deadline in order to avoid unnecessary conflict.

If the eligibility committee determines that the student's behavior is not a manifestation of the disabling condition, then the suspension can be carried out. The 10 day rule begins over again. If the action is a manifestation of the disabling condition, the eligibility committee might recommend a change in placement, changes to the IEP (such as the addition of a functional behavioral assessment and plan), or additional support. The suspension is then waived, because the changes that the eligibility committee makes indicate a causal relationship between the suspendable action and the student's disabling condition.

- Plan and implement an interim alternative educational setting (IAES) that will enable the student to participate in the general education curriculum along with the provisions to which the student is entitled in order to meet IEP goals and objectives

If the student was not involved with a dangerous situation, but was involved with a drug-policy violation, the district can place the student in an IAES for up to 45 days. After 45 days, however, the student returns to the previous placement.

If a student is suspended and the alternative placement is home instruction for a period of time, it is the responsibility of the teachers (with building administrator support) to make sure that work assignments are provided for the student. The student's work must be graded as though it were completed in school. It is *illegal* to deprive the suspended disabled student of the right to learn and/or make up work missed due to a suspension, as any alternative program constitutes a change in placement. Under IDEA, any change in placement negates issues from the previous placement (student begins with a clear record). While an action might have caused the change in placement, the student's disabling condition contributed to the need for a change, and was not under the control of the student due to his or her disability.

If administrators determine the student is *dangerous*, administrators can place the student in the IAES for up to 45 days. After 45 days, either the parents must agree to continue the IAES, or the student must be returned to the setting prior to the IAES.

If parents do not agree with the IAES, injunctive relief may be sought from a hearing officer. In order to be granted an injunction, the district must show the following:

- Current placement is likely to result in injury
- Current placement is appropriate
- Reasonable efforts were made to minimize risk
- IAES meets requirements delineated above.

If an injunction is granted, the student can be placed in IAES, and after another 45 days, the student either returns to previous placement or continues in the IAES.

DOCUMENTATION

Documentation is a *critical* component of the eligibility committee's role in identifying students with disabling conditions, in making recommendations for changes in programs and services, and in dealing with legal challenges. Building administrators must understand the importance of the documentation process and support both regular and special educators in gathering necessary data for eligibility meetings. Whether for initial reviews that specify classifications, special reviews for particular reasons (e.g., changes in programs or services), or annual reviews to discuss student programs and services for the next school year, reports to the committee by teachers who work with identified children are *required*. Districts typically have forms that include current grades, student strengths and weaknesses, and student social and behavioral needs (see sample forms that follow).

It is extremely important that the information presented on these documents be viewed as professional descriptions of factual information. If a legal challenge is presented at any point during a student's school attendance (or through age 21), these documents become part of the public record. Frequently, teachers perceive these forms as notes to a person or group of people, rather than an integral part of student records. Building leaders can support personnel by including forms and describing responsibilities to the eligibility committee process, as part of their building's teacher handbook.

Functional Behavioral Assessment

Student Name: **Date:**
Grade: **Completed by:**
Disability Classification:

Purpose of Behavioral Assessment (List child's presenting difficulties, describe in factual, behavioral terms, i.e., Johnny cursed at a teacher after being given directions, **not** Johnny was insubordinate)

The following information was reviewed as part of the assessment:

Check/Circle all that apply

_____ school records (discipline referrals, attendance, report card, cumulative folder, educational data, psychological, educational, related service evaluations)

_____ medical, social history, classroom observations, teacher summary reports

Identify Expectations in the Classroom

_____ classroom schedule posted and routines followed

_____ student works independently for ___ minutes, # times ___ throughout the day

_____ behavioral reinforcement used by: _______________

___ teacher provides ___ individual
___ group rewards ___ stickers
___ token reward system

Classroom Observation - completed by building evaluator (psychologist, guidance counselor, social worker, teacher)

Name ____________________________ Date________________

Functional Behavioral Assessment

Time ______________ Activity ______________________

Check observed behaviors:

Attentive	____ yes	____ no
Difficulties with transition	____ yes	____ no
Positive adult interaction	____ yes	____ no
Positive peer interaction	____ yes	____ no
Followed directions	____ yes	____ no
Communicated effectively	____ yes	____ no
Comprehended activity	____ yes	____ no
Seemed confused	____ yes	____ no
Demonstrated frustration	____ yes	____ no
Displayed aggressive behaviors (hit, kicked, etc.)	____ yes	____ no

Functional Behavioral Plan

Student Name: **Date:**
Grade: **Completed by:**
Disability Classification:

Identify behavior(s) in need of modification (up to 3)

State objective/goal/consequence in behavioral terms. For example, if a young child hits when frustrated —

Jane will use her voice to express she needs help instead of touching another person. She will be encouraged by:

- Receiving verbal praise when she verbally communicates wants/needs
- Receiving a sticker each time she raises her hand
- When she receives 5 stickers she earns computer time

If she hits a child, she will:

- be removed from activity (time out) for 3 minutes
- not earn a sticker for the activity
- have to apologize to student

Specify frequency/duration of behavioral plan (i.e.: 2 weeks, during morning activities)

Specify team members who developed/agreed to plan should include teacher(s), counselor, parent, and any other relevant school personnel (administrator if part of plan — i.e.: discipline referrals at secondary level)

- **Remember functional behavioral assessments and plan part of IEP and eligibility members discuss, approve and review!**

FINANCING SPECIAL EDUCATION

In order to understand the multifaceted issues associated with special education at the building and district levels, a brief review of financial issues commonplace in special education is important. Nationally, there is much misunderstanding regarding federal and state reimbursement of expenses to districts for providing special education services to children who need it. In 1975, when P.L. 94-142 was initiated, the federal government informed states that 40 percent of mandated special education services would be funded. Since that time, the federal government has funded between 4 and 7.5 percent of costs associated with special education (Chaikind, Danielson, and Brauen, 1993).

During hearings for IDEA in the 104th Congress (January, 1998), a bill introduced by Senate Majority Leader Trent Lott called for an increase in special education spending, which is currently up to 8 percent (Holmes, 1998). David Wolk, superintendent of schools in Rutland, Vermont, and a member of a panel of experts who testified before Congress, stated that across the nation, "special education mandated costs are among the few areas in the budget beyond our control." He further stated that accountability issues in maintaining schools of excellence is "increasingly threatened . . . by underfunded federal special education mandates." Judy Heumann, President Clinton's assistant secretary of special and rehabilitative services, declared that "data collection, annual LEA and SEA plans, as well as the many individual student requirements which must be documented, all result in a significant proportion of special education resources allocated to paper and process, rather than to students and families."

Between 1978 and 1998, funding levels were determined by the cost for students' individual services or by number of faculty hired to provide services for disabled students. *Individually calculated entitlements* were computed by assigning costs to the IEP needs for each child receiving services, combining those costs with the average cost for administrative, personnel, and instruction, and then developing a total state entitlement for special education. This is subtracted from federal aid provided, and the state provides the difference to the local district. This *fixed per-*

centage reimbursement was the formula 11 states used between 1978 and 1998.

Over two-thirds of the states have or are in the process of changing funding systems for the provision of special education services to students (Parrish, 1997). For example, North Carolina, Maryland, and Massachusetts revamped funding and provided *block grants*, which are based on the average daily enrollment of the school district. These block grants include special education funds. These sums were utilized to support all district programs, enabling districts to distribute resources as necessary. Many other states have begun to follow, moving away from funds tied to budget lines or type of service, so that "overidentification" or "mislabeling" is unnecessary for reimbursement (Parrish, 1997). Additional information regarding special education funding can be found in Appendix B.

It is important to note that there are benefits to the impending changes by states of financing special education. The federal government is now allowing funds previously marked for special education students only as a **shared resource** for a district, including program support for all students, collaboratively determined by the LEA. The ability to share resources for helping all students is a wonderful opportunity to develop and support student and staff program initiatives.

Roles of Stakeholders

Superintendents and Boards of Education

Superintendents and other central office administrators have the task of assuring board of education members, the community, and district administrators that legal entitlements for all students are provided in an appropriate manner. Expenditures, compliance, and discipline issues are the areas most commonly discussed and evaluated.

Due-process hearings need to be supported by superintendents and members of boards of education. When district administrators, responsible for special education processes and services for students with disabilities, recommend proceeding with a due-process challenge, it should be based on the fact that all avenues of mediation and compromise were exhausted (or parental insistence of pursuing legal action). There should be a strong likelihood that the district will prevail on the disputed issue. While no guarantee is possible, the superintendent and board members should be assured that a parental request is beyond entitlement, and that data from school records will support appropriateness of service and location. The district administrator must also ensure that all legal requirements of due process were complied with, as hearings are lost if documentation does not support regulatory compliance issues (notification letters, timelines, signatures as required, etc.).

Although central office administration and BOE members are concerned with the costs of a due-process challenge, if the hearing officer or court finds in favor of the district, the ultimate savings to a district might be substantial. Winning hearings provides support for district programs and can minimize further hearing requests. When families in a community know that there are services available for their disabled child based upon entitlements, families are more willing to compromise.

3

Educational Issues and Special Education

Legal compliance and regulatory issues were discussed in chapters 1 and 2. Although these issues pertain to all aspects of school, this chapter explores the concerns of school-based educators. These concerns include building-wide issues that impact all staff members:

- Scheduling
- Assessments
- Standards
- Grading
- Modifying instruction
- Fairness
- Paperwork.

These concerns impact schools, communities, parents, students, teachers, and administrators on a daily basis.

District Administration

District-wide administrators need to allocate resources of staff members and themselves to include time to talk with families and build trust. Parents often want what is "best" for their child and need help understanding the balance of school responsibility for appropriate educational services and other agency support available. If school counselors assist families in accessing additional agency resources, potential conflicts between educational services and habilitation services might be avoided.

Administrators given the responsibility of special education programs coordinate the eligibility process, placement process, services delivery, program location for students, parental due process, and faculty training. Knowledge of regulatory changes, legal processes, statewide initiatives of high standards and assessment, K–12 curricular changes and content at the local and state level, staff hiring, training and evaluation, consultation with all district administrators, parents, outside agencies, lawyers, advocates and post-school, transition service providers (vocational, college, work study programs) are all focused responsibilities of these key administrators.

These administrators report fiscal, legal, and educational information regarding students with disabilities to the BOE through superintendents on a regular basis. This occurs through federally mandated eligibility processes, state reporting through required data reports and grants, and on an as-needed basis for individual students.

Building issues such as student and class placement in school programs, scheduling, test modifications, grading and homework modifications, and behavior plans are topics frequently discussed and in need of reinforcement by district *and* building administrators. Staff in-service training in the areas of special education entitlements is an extensive task required of all administrators.

A survey was distributed to practicing administrators and teachers in 14 districts in 8 states. Data collected were the result of survey distribution to samples of school and district administrators in New York, Pennsylvania, Ohio, Indiana, California, Illinois, Florida, and New Jersey (Appendix C). The results are presented in Table 1.

TABLE 1. SPECIAL EDUCATION SURVEY RESPONDENTS, MAY 1998

Principals	Assistant Principals	Central Office	Teachers
70	18	22	32

N = 142

TABLE 2. TOP THREE CONCERNS REGARDING SPECIAL EDUCATION, 1998

Staff	Number One	Number Two	Number Three
Teachers	Equity/ Fairness	Grading/Test Modifications	Behavior/ Discipline
Principals/AP	Accountability Paperwork	Discipline	Instruction & Test Modifications
Central Office	Legal Compliance	Discipline Issues	Disruption of Instruction

The highest rated concerns of teachers, building-level administrators, and central office administrators are listed in Table 2.

As indicated by survey results, discipline, legal issues, and issues related to the delivery of instruction were highlighted concerns. Legal challenges and compliance, roles and responsibilities of administrators and faculty, accountability for curriculum and grading, inclusion, discipline, and parental roles emerged as areas of significance for practitioners.

BUILDING ADMINISTRATORS

Building principals are assigned the difficult task of ensuring that all students' needs are met. Schools want to be known for excellence, and student achievement outcomes are used as comparative measures of the ability of individual schools and districts to meet diverse challenges of educating all children.

Building administrators need to provide leadership to faculty, and support teachers in their ability to support students. Understanding student entitlements and communicating this knowledge effectively to teachers and parents support students, teacher, and children. When a building administrator is asked to mediate conflicts regarding discipline, equity, and fairness of test modification or grading, knowledge and communication are the keys to bringing understanding to all stakeholders.

ORGANIZATIONAL CHANGE

Change in schools has been researched extensively; it is difficult to organize systemic change without identifying the philosophy of the school (Wiles, 1993). Teachers tend to look at schools as highly structured domains, while students require and thrive in flexible settings. If students are viewed by adults as individuals with different learning styles, then they can take advantage of the developmental stages of children in order to create exciting and nurturing classroom environments.

Much has been learned from the business world regarding initiating and facilitating change in schools. Teachers can become disgusted and frustrated if building or district leaders try to implement a "new state-of-the-art" curriculum or philosophy immediately after it emerges. Trust in the organization weakens, as teachers feel as though they are asked to discard all their hard work and successes of the past, and start over with the new, improved curriculum, assessments or philosophy. Workdays lengthen as teachers struggle to learn, relearn, discard, and disengage themselves from past, present, and future practices.

Districts attempt to be leaders in change, at times forgetting the input of or impact on educators working to benefit the organization by teaching children on a daily basis. Miles (1965) stated that the health of an organization must focus on morale, innovation, resource utilization, autonomy, flexibility, and the ability to solve problems. Systematically, schools have evolved as cultures ruled by "subdivide and conquer," as specialists (gifted, remedial, and specialized programs) removed children from the general classroom environment and from each other. In doing so, teachers were told to prioritize and identify students for different programs and services. They became the gatekeepers of their classroom, as students came and went all day. Infrequently, the classroom teacher had the entire class to instruct, therefore the teacher spent much of the day teaching and reteaching material to students who were out of the room for various services. Teacher frustration increased as class size increased, the needs of students increased, but the school day and structure remained vastly the same. Teachers have no time to share their expertise, successes, or frustrations with each other in a constructive manner. Current practice reflects the situation reported by Lortie (1975): teaching is an isolated practice. The domain of each teacher is the classroom and little opportunity is presented for exchange of ideas. Lortie stated that teachers do not choose to acquire new standards to correct or reverse earlier impressions, ideas, or orientations. If educators have known this since the mid-1970s, why are we facing these same struggles at the beginning of the 21st century?

EDUCATIONAL REFORMS

A few of the educational reform movements between 1982 and 1998 that have had an impact on the teachers' trust of school systems include:

- Elements of instruction (Hunter, 1982)
- Cooperative learning (Johnson and Johnson, 1987; Slavin, 1986)
- Curriculum mapping (Hayes-Jacobs, 1989)
- Dimensions of learning (Marzano, 1992)
- Portfolio assessment (Vavrus, 1992)
- Multiple intelligences (Gardner, 1993)
- Learning styles (Price and Dunn, 1997)
- Brain research (Jensen, 1998)

It is no wonder that educators tire of the continual evolution of educational trends, fearing that as soon as a "new" concept is learned, acknowledged, and acquired, a replacement will be implemented. Frequent changes are one aspect of frustration. There are also curriculum and assessment changes, paperwork requirements that change, and the continual changing and challenging needs of students. It is not surprising that teachers are apprehensive about "volunteering" to work on a new project in school; the organization's commitment to continuity is debatable at best, based on track records of past experience.

Change is difficult. Change involves feelings of loss of comfortable and familiar patterns in schools (Brown and Moffett,

1999). Critical variables involved in school change include the building leaders' style in introducing change, the use of groups and committees, and rewards (Wiles, 1993). Factors that support people in organizational change include (Byham, 1988):

- Responsibility
- Trust
- Teams
- Praise
- Recognition for ideas
- Direction
- Support
- Communication

When one change occurs in a school organization, a domino effect results, because an alteration in one part of a system usually causes something else to change. The most successful changes occur at the building level, because the key for stability and continuity is within the building organization (Wiles, 1993). Change creates confusion, conflict, and feelings of incompetence (Deal, 1994). Everyone begins at ground zero, because previous successes are not necessarily a part of the change process.

Too often, systemic school change is initiated from the top down, resulting in confusion or chaos as the focus filters down to the building level. Anyone who has played the game of "telephone" can recall how a simple message changes as it is whispered from one to another, and how the message is altered each time it is passed on. At the end of the game, everyone laughs when the last person states an unrecognizably garbled message—significantly different from the initial message.

In schools, the way messages change might differ as the hierarchical continuum is followed, adding complexity to the confusion as building and district leaders interpret messages from central office administrators differently. The role of the building principal is vitally important to faculty when change occurs. When a building leader is supportive of change, faculty members attempt to support change. When building administrators are negative about change, they encourage faculty to ignore or refuse change.

Too often an inordinate amount of time is focused on strategic planning, prior to initiating change. A balance between training and doing must be achieved. Spending too much time in advanced planning is a mistake, for as people try things out, take risks, retry, and develop flexible options, people become more skilled, ideas evolve, and the shared commitment to the process becomes stronger (Fullan, 1993).

In order for schools to develop the ongoing, necessary gains for students, adults (administration, BOE members, teachers, and parents) must experience and endure the challenges that come from restructuring and rethinking designs in educational systems (Sizer, 1991). Allowing teachers to become interactive professionals supports continuous school improvement (Fullan and Hargreaves, 1996). People need to feel valued and connected to the change process. Building and district level support must be more than empty words.

Planning for constructive change requires refocusing on change for a positive purpose, not to "fix" an isolated element that is not working. As Dr. J. Bruce McKenna (1998) presented at a workshop on educational change, the first step is to identify the ideal. Think of what the desired result is, and work from that premise. All stakeholders must have input into defining the ideal, based on the stated purpose for change. The next shared task is to define problems in terms of the objectives and have the change process involve everyone as a planner. Various steps might require different levels of involvement, but it is important that all constituents are involved in the change process through the planning, implementation, and evaluation stages. The goal is to encourage people to establish goals and objectives within the given framework and work collaboratively toward systemic change. Reorienting focus on change as something that can be accomplished in a positive manner enables people to challenge strategies and construct new goals. Focus should not be directed toward what was wrong before, but on the exciting and new directions that can be taken to improve results.

The role of building-based educational leaders is to facilitate change with political awareness. Leaders must be aware that the needs and goals of an educational organization, as perceived by faculty, do not always result in the best decisions for students. Shared decision making (SDM) and site-based management (SBM) are terms frequently used to describe collaborative ways for faculty in schools to have input to educational reforms. Researchers identified benefits of SDM and SBM as processes that enable staff to solve problems together, assisting teachers in taking control of the educational arena, and reducing the isolation teachers feel (Kentta, 1997; Kilgore and Webb, 1997; Villars, 1991; Darling-Hammond and McLaughlin, 1995).

Principals must create and build upon the concept of sharing expertise among members of the school, rather than depending on "outside experts" who are summoned to solve problems. The question becomes how a principal can initiate change and maintain a balance that benefits students and staff, while supporting the political and community goals reflected by organizational demands. Change is driven by the complexity of needs: standards, assessments, politics, student versus adult needs. There is and always will be a politically driven hierarchy of power in educational systems. How power transcends and supports positive change for staff, students, and families is always evolving.

Decision makers should be representative of the school community, as appropriate. In order to build and maintain a positive professional culture in schools, constituents who will be affected by change should have a voice. Input should be gathered and shared. Options should be discussed. Final decisions will not make everyone happy, but participation in the process and being heard will help build support in the change process.

SCHEDULING

Scheduling daily events in a building is a complicated task—one area all stakeholders identified as a concern. Whether block scheduling, traditional scheduling, or flexible scheduling is implemented in a building, conflicts occur and not all constituents will be pleased. Changes further contribute to frustration.

Frequently, changes involve special education students and staff, because scheduling needs change based upon the changing needs of services for identified students.

In a comprehensive school program for students with disabilities, creating teams that include special education teachers, content teachers, and all elective teachers can be a monumental task. The core subject areas of math, science, reading and English, and social studies should be key to scheduling and avoiding conflict. For example, in an elementary school, if a student with a disability is in a separate class for math instruction, the class should occur when nondisabled peers are being instructed in math in their classroom. Regulations specify that primary part-time special education instruction cannot exclude a student with a disability from participation in other content areas. Additionally, students who receive special education services in math must be grouped with students in the *same* subject area. In an elementary school where there might be ten students placed in four different third-grade classrooms, the four third-grade teachers must cooperate so that the students who receive math instruction in special education classes can be scheduled efficiently. This obviously calls for significant coordination, which also impacts other building schedules. Physical education, art, music, and library and media often share staff, and flexibility control does not remain in one building. One solution for part of the building schedule can create havoc for another.

At the secondary level, special education content classes need to be offered in core curriculum areas required for graduation. Requirements might vary by state, but all states have adopted high standards as benchmarks for demonstrated student achievement. In a traditional secondary schedule, each class is a set period of time. Scheduling special education classes depends on the timing and scheduling of vocational programs and having enough (at least two in large buildings) core subject classes at each grade level of both inclusive and separate class offerings. Electives at the secondary level typically offer a greater degree of flexibility, and more options in course selection exist, which meet elective requirements.

Block Scheduling and Schools-within-a-School (House Plans)

These philosophies have gained popularity as ways for schools to better manage student and staff needs. Although these concepts encourage communication among teams of teachers and encourage collaboration and shared decision-making, administrators and teachers must still deliver appropriate special education services. The IEP for each child *must* be complied with, regardless of building scheduling problems or programs. For example, if an IEP dictates that a student receive 40 minutes of math a day for a disabled student, and the team in a block decides not to do math for one week, a potential problem emerges.

This does not mean that creativity and options do not exist. It is important to know and understand the concept of allocated time for a subject delineated in an IEP. If the average time per week is two hours per core subject, and the average instructional time is met, the school could easily defend itself against a challenge. However, if a student with a disability needs routine and repetition due to the nature and severity of the existing disability, fewer changes to daily schedules would be defensible.

As in all other areas of education, applying a balance of common sense and doing what is good for student learning is the common goal. There are a limited number of hours, days, and weeks students spend in school, and when a student participates in one option, such as chorus, the choice prohibits participation in something else that is going on at the same time. Reasonable changes to routines and student schedules are expected. For example, field trips and assembly programs change school schedules and students with disabilities are entitled to participate.

Clustering/Grouping Students

When students with disabilities are clustered in classroom sections, this can assist the scheduling process in both elementary and secondary settings. Students can be assigned to classrooms based on level and type of service. For example, if there are 12 students with mild to moderate disabilities in fifth grade, planning to cluster six students in two different sixth-grade classes for the following year will allow for scheduling options that would not exist if two students were placed in each of six sections. Content teachers, special education teachers, and electives teachers can plan activities by coordinating schedules with a few colleagues, rather than with many, and building schedules will have less conflict.

TEACHER TRAINING

Identifying needs and supporting faculty in the implementation of change is a shared goal of teachers. Building leaders should encourage staff participation in district-wide training opportunities. Principals should encourage a cycle of improvement through innovative practices, risk-taking, feedback, and reflection.

There is a perceived notion among teachers that the training and certification of special education teachers differs significantly from that of regular (content) education teachers. This was true in terms of teacher certification in content areas at the secondary level, but was not true in major aspects of elementary or special education teacher-training programs at colleges or universities.

Between the late 1970s and the late 1980s, teacher-training programs were geared toward elementary or secondary education. Special education programs included a few (typically two or three) courses pertaining to differences, specifying a disabling condition for one or two classes, and an extra class in psychology. For example, some states have required that an "expert" in learning disabilities or mental retardation have as few as six credit hours (two courses) beyond the same elementary or secondary teacher training program. Few professionals would agree that expertise can be imparted in two college courses. However, many classroom teachers with numerous years of experience believe a newly certified, inexperienced special education teacher knows the "magic" of dealing with children in special education while it is clearly the experience of the classroom teacher that provides the needed expertise.

Teacher-training programs in special education for the secondary level were geared more toward providing strategies and techniques for delivering instruction, rather than focusing on a specific content area. However, most of the methods classes were the same methods classes required of other teacher-training programs. Again, a few additional classes were required in psychology. Practical application of behavior modification might have been the focus of one class, but one course does not make an "expert."

Clearly, experience with children teaches teachers more than a course or two in a college program. States are beginning to recognize important certification issues, and colleges and universities are beginning to provide teacher-training programs without separating special education from content teachers. Many states are instituting a new certification structure that will be effective in September 2003, as a result of the changing focus on effective teaching from colleges, universities, and practitioners. The Council for Exceptional Children (CEC, 1995) suggested that international standards for the preparation and certification of special education teachers should include the following:

Common Core Knowledge and Skills

- Knowledge of the philosophical, historical, and legal foundations of special education
- Understanding the characteristics of diverse learners
- Instructional content
- Communication and collaborative partnerships
- Planning and management of the teaching and learning environment
- Managing student behavior and social skills.

Specialists

- After core, areas of expertise based on disability classification to enhance professional knowledge and guide practice.

Many states strongly emphasize similar new teacher certification requirements (e.g., New York, Maryland, and California). The focus of change can be summarized by having all teachers be specialists within a developmental level (early childhood, childhood, special education—childhood or adolescence), a core subject specialist, and have a content specific endorsement. The specialist areas will require field placements in all levels covered by the certificate, and both elementary and secondary level instructors, regardless of special area, must have an additional content specialty (NYS Education Department, Fall, 1997).

Many states are changing teacher certification requirements so that teachers are content-, age-, and disability-specialists. In New England, a consortium representing Connecticut, Maine, Massachusetts, New Hampshire, Rhode Island, and Vermont met and developed a common set of competencies for teachers between 1994 and 1997. Certification requirements in these states were changed to meet new standards for teacher certification. Roles of educators are changing in the following manner as reflected in the various certification proposals:

Different expectations

- Multiple teaching roles. Teachers must have the ability to work with disabled students, lead collaborative efforts, and be active consultants in the educational process. Teachers must also change from a label-based system, comprising 13 disabling conditions, to being educators of mildly, moderately, or severely disabled children. They must also have a subject area endorsement, and an age-level certification.
- Different roles for learners. Students would no longer be labeled as having 1 of 13 disabilities. Rather, the plan for their education would be developed in conjunction with students' levels of disability.

Teacher preparation

- Instructional leadership. Teachers must learn how to facilitate change in an organization.

- Communication. Educators need to learn how to communicate positively and collaboratively in a variety of situations.
- Teaching strategy development. Education departments must provide graduates with methodologies for addressing a diverse student population with varied disabilities.
- Curriculum development. Teachers need to be knowledgeable of curriculum frameworks and how to assess mastery of the curriculum. Special education teachers are no longer isolated from mainstream colleagues and students. Student outcomes become shared goals.

Teacher awareness

- Broad experiences. Teacher preparation programs must emphasize the importance of visiting general-education classrooms as well as classes for special education. Teachers need to learn to respect each others' roles in students' lives.
- Emphasis on collaboration. Teacher education programs need to prepare teachers for team teaching, and co-teaching—to work together to make it work.

When IDEA was reauthorized in 1997, federal statutes specified that all teachers be prepared to work with disabled students of all levels. The 1997 reauthorization emphasized that the disabled are entitled to receive instruction in regular classrooms when appropriate, and that all disabled students receive instruction in the general education curriculum. Given these emphases it makes sense for certification requirements to change. All teachers must have content knowledge and be prepared to work with diverse populations in their classrooms. College and university teacher-training programs are focusing on preparing teachers, not separating special education and regular-education teachers. The acknowledgment that all teachers must be prepared to provide instruction to all students is a significant issue as we move into the 21st century.

Teachers should consider that "special education" is not as different as it is sometimes perceived. Teachers provide instruction to heterogeneous groups all the time, by identifying student strengths and weaknesses in different skill areas. When "labels" are involved (gifted, remedial, special education), the label often leads people to believe that "someone else" (a specialist) is responsible for instructing the labeled child. The bureaucratic educational system perpetuates this belief, because over the last decade, teacher certification courses and programs were developed to support the separation of students by labels and services. However, it is in the best interest of the students and staff to realign the way children's learning needs can be met with shared expertise.

In a 1997 study, 61 percent of all classroom teachers at the elementary level reported that they had no training in teaching gifted students (Culross, 1997). A review of the literature found the *same* suggestions were proposed for teaching gifted students and special education students, including restructuring the regular classroom to accommodate diverse learners, modifying the curriculum, instructional practices, and grading (Skrtic, 1991; Dettmer, 1993; Jackson, 1993; Maker, 1995).

At the middle level, the same similarities between educating academically gifted and special education students are evident in the literature as well. General educational concepts supported by middle-level education experts (Merenbloom, 1998) are synonymous with the goals and objectives of special education. *This We Believe* (National Middle School Association, 1995) focuses on various teaching and learning approaches, including engaging learners with hands-on experiences, cooperative groups, technology, and the promotion of higher-level thinking skills, decision making, and creativity. Building a caring relationship between adults and students is a goal of advisory-advisee programs that are well supported in middle-school philosophy.

Teachers should view students and develop an understanding of details of development of social relationships with peers and adults, and expectations. The teacher becomes a liaison for a small group of students in school and between home and school as appropriate. The opportunity for students to be connected with an adult in a secondary school assists students and teachers in building a trusting and respectful relationship. Students with disabilities often need to make personal connections, because previous school experiences might have been frustrating and difficult.

All students want to be valued members of their school society. In order for teachers to meet the diverse needs of students, they must acknowledge the need for change, focus on future visions, and work collaboratively to maximize collegial strengths and knowledge. They must have administration support and the resources to implement, evaluate, and facilitate positive change on behalf of the student within the process of restructuring efforts. A survey was conducted of teachers' use of curriculum modifications for meeting needs of diverse learners in the classroom (Appendix D). The survey is a modification of one distributed by Drs. Joyce Meikamp and Steve Russell (University of West Virginia) at a YAI conference in New York, NY, in May 1998 (used with permission). Teachers from New York, Indiana, Pennsylvania, and New Jersey completed the survey, representing a range of years of experience (1–11+) and instructional grade level (primary to high school). All respondents indicated whether they were regular classroom or special education teachers. The results are presented in Table 3. The purpose of the survey was to assess the willingness of teachers to use or consider using alternatives that made sense for helping students demonstrate knowledge.

Survey results indicated that both regular and special educators use cooperative groups frequently (22). Using untimed tests (18), pairing low-ability students with peer tutors for study, review, or test preparation (11), and allowing students extra time to complete assignments (12) are other modifications both groups of teachers use. Highlighting essential information on worksheets (10), providing supplemental content on a lower readability level than the textbook (1), previewing questions and providing guides for upcoming class discussions (5), administering practice tests (13), assigning alternative homework (19), and selecting fewer concepts for lower functioning students to learn (21) are used by more than half the respondents in both groups.

TABLE 3. CURRICULUM MODIFICATION SURVEY RESULTS, JUNE 1998

	Special education teachers (46 respondents)		Regular education teachers (70 respondents)	
	Use	Would Use	Use	Would Use
1.	82	7	67	19
2.	65	15	41	36
3.	65	9	37	29
4.	39	24	17	21
3.	74	15	63	16
4.	22	41	14	40
7.	39	24	37	13
8.	17	41	4	29
9.	37	37	3	27
10.	87	11	67	17
11.	76	15	94	6
12.	96	2	94	3
13.	61	22	58	11
14.	61	7	30	26
15.	52	22	27	39
16.	11	46	10	43
17.	11	46	4	46
18.	78	11	59	6
19.	72	13	61	13
20.	30	9	43	7
21.	63	11	73	10
22.	87	7	91	3

Allowing students to record answers to essay questions (16), recording content from the textbook for poor readers (6), and using recorded tests with poor readers (17) were used by few members of either group. Both groups, however, indicated they would consider using this tool at approximately the same rate (40–46 percent of respondents).

Many teachers who responded to the survey indicated that they would consider using some of the suggested modifications.

Regular educators disliked permitting students to view films independently or listen to tapes outside of class (9), allowing students to record class discussions or lectures (8), or providing outlines of lectures (4). Fewer than 40 percent of all teachers said they "used" or "would consider using" these methods.

Special educators indicated they dislike allowing students with disabilities to work on other assignments during the lesson (20). Assigning alternative in-class work is the only method that fewer than 40 percent of special educators said they use or would consider using.

TEAM TEACHING

The "innovative" practice of team teaching was identified in the early 1970s (Lortie, 1975). Team teaching is frequently associated with inclusion and collaboration for teaching diverse learners, as a "new" concept in the 1990s. Many ideas in education are recycled in accordance with societal change. In the 1970s, this "innovative paradigm shift" occurred as open classrooms and individualized programmed instruction developed as a way of breaking down segregating *walls* in school buildings. In the 1990s, this "innovative paradigm shift" occurred as a way of breaking down segregating *labels* of children.

In order for schools to support teachers in a team-teaching, collaborative environment, teachers must have time to meet and communicate with one another. Words that are not supported by actions cause many innovative ideas to fall by the wayside, as teachers need to feel their time and commitment is valued by the school district. Shared planning time is an essential component when teachers work together with shared students. Davis (1995) indicated that when people work in groups, more ideas are generated, because the exchange of ideas with colleagues generates even more ideas. Team planning facilitates effective communication, as ideas are valued by colleagues. The team begins to function as a group, developing common goals and objectives. Frustration leads to creative thinking, and challenges become shared problem-solving sessions. Davis (1995) reported that effective problem solvers demonstrate skills in seeing the ultimate goal, support change by creating webs of knowledge and by setting flexible goals. As one goal or objective is reached, others are modified or achieved.

When teachers implement cooperative teaching techniques, students develop as cooperative learners. Educators across disciplines agree that children learn by doing. Teachers can effectively teach by modeling and providing opportunities for students to be actively engaged in the classroom. Classrooms are mini-societies in which students learn throughout grades K–12 how to be members of a democratic system. Societal issues will be reflected in each classroom, and teachers and students need to learn how to function together for a shared purpose.

Building and district leaders must create a professional atmosphere for teachers and support staff. Sergiovanni and Starrett (1983) supported the concept of teamwork and stakeholder empowerment, in order to allow teachers to be catalysts for change. If teachers are not supportive of change due to systemic organizational issues, productive change for instructional improvement will be blocked.

Collaborative cultures acknowledge and encourage purposeful teacher input, and building leaders can sustain this type of working environment productively (Fullan and Hargreaves, 1996). Facilitating discussions, disagreements, and resolutions build bonds of organizational support for all participants.

All teachers want their students to succeed, but teachers become frustrated by the lack of time they have to develop and implement alternatives. Team teaching supports the notion that planning is an important commodity. The following worksheet might help guide planning sessions between collaborating teachers. Use the information requested to identify issues proactively for teachers to use in lesson planning and delivery.

In order to adapt instruction, curriculum objectives must be clearly stated. Begin with the skills you want students to achieve, and then plan backward from that point. A wide variety of materials enables teachers to meet the most learning styles more effectively. Students want to demonstrate their abilities rather than identify their weaknesses. If the classroom enables students to learn in multiple ways and if information is presented to stu-

COLLABORATIVE PLANNING GUIDE

Date ________ Time __________ Topic ___________

Attendees

____

____

List five important issues related to topic:

1.
2.
3.
4.
5.

List needed curricular materials:

List concerns regarding implementation:

List roles of each teacher in planning and implementing lesson:

Identify follow-up activities and identify teachers who will provide each to students:

dents in many ways, everyone is successful and frustration can be avoided.

GRADING

One of the most controversial issues associated with collaborative teaching between special and regular educators pertains to grading student work with fairness and equity. Frequently teachers (both special and content) claim that it is unfair for students to be measured differently; they resist test modifications for students, refuse to modify test length and format, and play the "equity" card. At the secondary level, content teachers often state that "if special education students are in my class, they must be able to pull their weight." Statements like these are detrimental to students and teachers, and building administrators need to be able to support the legally correct answer.

Students with disabilities are *entitled* to all modifications the eligibility committee determines to be appropriate, and *only* the committee can make that determination. It does not matter what the personal opinion of a teacher or administrator is. As building leader, you must promote and publicize this fact or you will put yourself in a position that *cannot* be legally supported.

Modifications are based on the nature and severity of a student's disability. The purpose of leveling the playing field is to allow students to demonstrate knowledge. I recently heard a special education teacher of an elementary-aged student describe a situation where the student, who is learning disabled and cannot spell due to her disability, took a social studies test. It was apparent from written responses that the student was able to demonstrate knowledge in the content area. However, the classroom teacher insisted that the student could have "tried harder" and did not want to give the student full credit for test responses. After a discussion, the classroom teacher asked the *parent* whether the child should get full or partial credit for responses given. The special education teacher's explanation of test modifications did not satisfy the classroom teacher, nor did the legality of providing test modifications as an educational responsibility. The parent must have wondered about being given the choice and could have raised a legal challenge. Disabled and non-disabled students need to be graded fairly. Equity is not always equal, and teachers need assistance understanding this at times. As building principal, there are ways to help teachers understand this concept.

A student's IEP indicates applicable test modifications, and both regular and special educators are responsible for ensuring that they are followed. All teachers have access to IEPs, but typically special education teachers summarize necessary information from the IEPs in a written statement to other teachers the student comes in contact with. The forms provided in chapter 5 are samples used by districts for informing teachers of IEP information.

IMPLEMENTING TEST MODIFICATIONS IN REGULAR CLASSES

A critical issue involving test modifications, grading, and special education students is this: Many educators believe that if students participate in regular education classes, they should be held to the same standard, despite knowledge of their disability. As mentioned in chapter 2, students are not mainstreamed, or included in regular classes, in order to negate students' disabilities. When educators, who are aware of students' disabilities, demand that special students be subject to the same standards as non-disabled students, it is tantamount to asking a deaf child to hear, a blind child to see, or a wheelchair-bound student to walk. A student *should* participate in regular education classes, if, with *appropriate modifications,* the student can learn and demonstrate knowledge. Test modifications are determined by the eligibility committee and are the responsibility of *both* special and regular classroom teachers. Modifications *must* be carried out in order to comply with state and federal regulations. Many educators do not realize that modifications can be approved for students by the building principal for *any* student if appropriate. (For example, New York's Part 100 regulations grant authority to building principals to determine appropriate modifications for students.)

The following exercise has been an effective activity with adult learners in graduate classes and workshops:

Activity One

Please transcribe the following paragraph. It is a timed activity—you have 3 minutes.

-leefnu dna errazib rehtar mees yam ti hguohtlA
teem ot kcul doog saw ti deveileb elpoep ynam, yadot gni
no nemrehsif .ksat tnatropmi emos no nehw toidi na
enoyna fo htap eht ssore ot that dleh ralucitrap
rieht ot gniog nehw deenalabnu yllatnem saw ohw
luffsseccus dna efas a erusne dluow staob
that si noititsrepus siht fo nigiro eht.egayov
etipsed dna "roop s'doG" era elpeop hcuslla
yaw now rieht ni deeselb era snoitatimil rieht
dlo ni that,oot, eton ot gnitseretni is tI
."desselb" tnaem yllis drow eht, hsilgnE

Answer Key

Although it may seem rather bizarre and unfeeling today, many people believed it was good luck to meet an idiot when on some important task. Fisherman in particular held that to cross the path of anyone who was mentally unbalanced when going to their boats would ensure a safe and successful voyage. The origin of this superstition is that all such people are "God's poor" and despite their limitations are blessed in their own way. It is interesting to note, too, that in old English, the word silly meant "blessed."

Students with a learning disability might perceive information as the teacher perceives both the paragraph as presented and as transcribed. Adults who completed this three-minute activity using their non-dominant hand at various workshops conducted by the author indicated how they felt. Some of their comments included: "hand hurt," "slow," "no control," "lessened concentration level," "got a headache," "eye strain," and "stress."

Feeling less than competent when you know you are a bright and capable person is a frustrating experience that is typical of learning-disabled students. Understanding how a student feels may assist teachers in their personal views of fairness in grading.

Fifty percent of classroom teachers adapt individual grading criteria for non-disabled students (Bursuck et al., 1996). Adaptations to grading include grading for improvement, effort, and assigning separate grades for answers and thought processes in determining answers (Munk and Bursuck, 1998). These researchers reported that teachers vary in which grades they modify and suggested that school districts establish policies on grading, which lists appropriate ways for teachers to modify grades. If the policy determination is done with teacher and administrative input, and stated in teacher handbooks, teachers might perceive grading options as modifications for any student they, as professionals, determine is appropriate. This would minimize the perception that students with disabilities are treated unfairly and enable all students to demonstrate knowledge in a variety of ways with teacher support.

Special education teachers are specialists in adaptations for students with differing needs. They can help the content teacher by preparing:

- Study guides for content
- Consultations for lesson presentation
- Multisensory experiences (lessons presented with auditory, visual, and tactile aspects)
- Outlined chapters
- Highlighted content
- Test format revisions

SUGGESTIONS FOR TEST MODIFICATIONS IN THE CLASSROOM

- Provide tests with fewer questions for *full credit* (e.g., 10 problems instead of 20)
- Vary test formats depending on individual need of student (short-answer, multiple-choice, essay, oral, open-book, take-home)

- Present limited material on one page (spacing issues)
- Allow students to demonstrate knowledge in alternative ways (orally—on tape, dictated to teacher or computer)
- Read test directions to entire class (often done)
- Present step-by-step directions in a short, simple format (for *any* student to use)
- Provide completed examples
- Provide concrete manipulatives for student use (chalkboard, computer)
- Use cooperative learning activities for projects that demonstrate student learning
- Have students work in pairs

GRADING HOMEWORK ASSIGNMENTS WITH MODIFICATIONS

Teachers should be flexible in determining modifications for homework. All children should be responsible for homework assignments, but remember and remind staff that the *purpose* of homework is to reinforce learned or taught skills and to prepare for learning activities so that knowledge can be *demonstrated* and skills *reinforced*. In determining appropriate homework assignments:

- Never assume that all children should complete the same quantity of work.
- Always assume the assignments need modification.
- Break the assignment down into sequential steps.
- Teach first, and then use homework for review to check for student understanding.
- Provide copies of overheads used during lesson for student notes.
- Give time during period for assignment to be copied down or provide a written copy to students who have difficulty writing or copying from the board.

A TEACHER GUIDE FOR CLASSROOM MODIFICATIONS

Organizational Skills

- Learners with mild disabilities need consistency; therefore teachers should establish a daily routine in their classrooms.
- Make sure the student's work area is clear of unnecessary material that might be distracting.
- Have students keep an assignment notebook and calendar of future assignments. This teaches students organization and responsibility.
- Have review time at the beginning of the period to relate previous information to present lecture. Also, allow time at the end of the period to summarize and answer questions. This ties the lesson together.
- When assigning projects, provide samples of finished projects along with directions for guidance.
- Be consistent in posting homework assignments. Choose a particular portion of the board on which to write this information.
- Keep a list of class and homework assignments for students to check periodically.
- Always tell students about changes in routine of schedules, so they will know what to expect.
- Establish a procedure to prevent misplacement of assignments. Have students place completed work in folders, trays, notebooks, etc.
- Keep directions short and simple and write them on the board, so students can refer to them.
- Provide a regular schedule of "cleaning house" (desks, lockers, storage areas) to help students with organization.
- Use asterisks or circles to distinguish questions that require an implied fact. This will keep students from wasting time trying to find exact answers in the book.

- Provide or help students with a materials checklist of items needed for class.
- Teach students an organized approach to reading. For example, the SQ3R approach can help some students: Study, Question, Read, Recite, Review.

Test Taking Aids

Before taking a test, it is beneficial for students with disabilities to have a systematic procedure for studying and taking tests. Students need to know how to study for tests, what to concentrate on, how to interpret questions, and the mechanics of test taking. With test-taking skills, students will be able to study effectively and demonstrate their knowledge of the subject on a test.

PREPARING, REVIEWING, AND TAKING TESTS

Preparing. Devise a test information guide that includes the following:

- Test date.
- Chapters to be covered.
- Lecture outlines or recorded lectures.
- Additional information covered (filmstrips, etc.).
- Types of questions.
- Specific teacher instructions.
- Number of questions and point values.

Reviewing

- Help the student use the SQ3R method (Study, Question, Read, Recite, Review).
- Issue vocabulary words and definitions.
- Work with the student to allocate time for studying. (Use a calendar and set study times.)
- Hold a question and review session before tests.

- Have the student write questions that surface during reading.
- Fill in the gaps on a list of test information.
- Review notes, concentrating on areas that are unclear to the student.
- Help the student meet with a partner and review material orally to detect areas of weakness
- Concentrate on recognition and association for objective tests.
- Provide a study guide reviewing all materials which will be tested.

USES AND ADAPTATIONS FOR THE TAPE RECORDER

- Students may work at their own pace.
- Teachers can prepare tapes of spelling words, math facts, and science lessons that correspond to worksheets or other activities to provide sequential instruction.
- Teachers can make tapes of directions for complicated activities on textbook assignments.
- Class discussions can be taped and later evaluated by class members or the teacher.
- Classroom lectures can be taped for those students who cannot take notes or for students who are absent.
- Students can listen to a taped story and follow in their books by using a pointer or their finger to equate the printed word with the sound.
- Tape recorders can be used for reinforcement of correct pronunciation of words in English class.
- Record study questions at the ends of chapters, pausing for student responses.
- Record chapters and activities in books for students with learning disabilities.

Developing Student Guides

Some students learn quickly the skills involved in demonstrating their knowledge on tests. You can help other students demonstrate their knowledge on tests by providing a guide to skills and methods for taking tests. The following represent some of the techniques you can teach all students about taking tests.

TAKING TESTS

- Read directions and underline key phrases and words; then do the same as you read each question.
- Answer questions that you are sure of first.
- Place a check by questions that you are unsure of and skip these.
- Review a test and check answers after finished.
- Place an "X" on pages that you have reviewed so you do not waste time.
- Find out the following:
  - What is on the test.
  - What was on the previous test.
  - Set up and follow study procedures.
  - Know the test terms
  - Develop a positive mental attitude.

DIFFERENT TYPES OF TEST ITEMS

Different types of test items require different attack strategies. Help students develop skills for responding to each kind of test question.

Multiple Choice

- Formulate an answer after reading the questions and *before* reading the answers.
- Read each answer as though it were true or false.
- Draw a line through inappropriate answers.

- Know the rules of grammar, such as when to use "a" and "an" to determine if the answer will begin with a vowel or consonant sound.
- Use other questions as cues.

Matching

- Begin with the first term in the column and scan the other column for the answer.
- Write the answer in the blank and cross off that choice in your answer column.
- Skip terms or items that you are unsure of and return to them after all questions are answered.

True or False

- Become familiar with the vocabulary of these questions: all, some, never, always, every, none, sometimes.
- Look at all parts of the questions; all parts must be accurate to be true.
- Use other questions on the test as cues to possible answers.

Essay

- Develop a rough outline and verbalize thoughts while studying.
- Develop a key-points outline, put main ideas in order, and then fill in the facts.
- Answer an opinion question with the way you feel about the questions.

RESPONSIBILITIES OF THE SPECIAL EDUCATION TEACHER

- Provide classroom teachers with student data from the IEP (see sample forms in chapter 5).
- Discuss students' needs at least once a week during daily planning period.

- Inform classroom teachers of any changes in IEPs, medication, student stresses (family, job, etc.).
- Share achievement scores with classroom teachers.
- Be available for parent-teacher conferences as a team member with classroom teachers.
- Invite classroom teachers to scheduled meetings.
- Discuss test modifications, grading, and curriculum modifications for students.
- Modify lessons, tests, and study guides, as needed for students.
- Grade shared students collaboratively.
- Communicate!

RESPONSIBILITIES OF THE REGULAR-EDUCATION TEACHER

- Be aware of individual students who receive special education support services.
- Meet to discuss students' needs at least once a week during shared planning sessions.
- Keep the special education teacher informed of upcoming tests and projects, so that the special education teacher can work with the student to prepare, plan, and complete assignments.
- Make sure teachers have copies of worksheets, texts, and exams, so that modifications can be made proactively for student support.
- Inform the special education teacher of student concerns.
- Be available for team parent conferences.
- Grade shared students collaboratively.
- Communicate!

As federal and state regulations move toward higher standards for all students, student outcomes and measures of accountability dictate curricular changes. National requirements for standards in reading, math, and writing have created statewide reforms of curricula and assessment. Between 1998 and 2000, many of these changes became requirements for all students—including those with disabilities—to achieve a high school diploma. Minimum competency tests that were mandatory in each state over the past eight years are being replaced by outcome-based measurements with higher standards, established as graduation requirements for all students.

Measuring student progress toward goals or objectives and evaluation that uses data and standards to judge quality of progress, are integral to statewide initiatives for higher standards for all students across our nation. In 1983, *A Nation at Risk* was published, identifying mediocrity as a guiding principle of the American educational system. In 1998, educators were moving toward a system of higher expectations and standards for all students. The central failings of American education involves "mediocre quality, weak performance, low efficiency, and slack productivity" (Finn, 1998). The need for change was identified long ago, with substantial change finally emerging 15 years later.

Assessment of student progress is critical for both students and teachers. Feedback for students is important, relative, and desired. Using *curriculum-based assessment* is appropriate to assess skill acquisition. The use of familiar words and concepts enables students to minimize test anxiety and produce evidence of skills learned. Teachers can evaluate student progress and identify areas in the curriculum that need additional review and instruction.

Portfolio assessment as an accurate measure of student progress is another way to assess skill acquisition. Teachers continually evaluate effects of instruction to ensure students' progress at acceptable rates (Wesson and King, 1996). Teaching students how to learn and thinking about how learning occurs is imbedded in portfolio assessment. Students have input into what goes into their portfolios and connect items to curriculum objectives. Students reflect on learning activities and provide feedback for themselves and teachers in doing so. IEP goals and objectives can be measured and modified using this type of cumulative assessment. Continuous monitoring of progress and identification of areas in need of remediation are valuable tools that portfolio assessment provides.

Both content teachers and special education teachers are responsible for evaluating progress on report cards and IEPs. Federal regulations *require* that IEP goals and objectives are updated and communicated to parents *at least as often* as regular education updates student progress. This means that each time report cards are sent home, IEP goals and objectives must be updated and sent to parents. This can be in various formats: copies of updated IEPs, progress reports, summary boxes on report cards (samples of which are included in chapter 5).

PARENTS

Parents expect that their children go to school to be educated. Qualities of respect, responsibility, caring, dignity, and safety foster a positive learning and teaching environment.

Family and school partnerships encourage communication as a key between school and home. Progress reports, report cards, conferences, open houses, and other school programs that encourage parental support of students and teachers should be presented throughout the school year.

When parents think their input is valued, the support generated is invaluable. School districts across the country have involved parents beyond that which the PTA offers and encourage various building-level and district-level leadership teams. These teams enable stakeholders to meet and discuss building and district issues, providing insights and input to programs and policy development.

The conflict parents frequently face is trying to maintain a balance between their children's right to privacy and ensuring that entitlements are available for their children. For example, students need test modifications, but parents do not want their children pulled out of class; a child needs extra classes for assistance, but the parents do not want their child to miss any other course.

There are a finite number of hours in a school day. Anytime a child needs an additional subject, be it an advanced or remedial or special education course, another subject might be sacrificed. The difficulty is in making the choice that makes the most sense for each student. Parents need to understand the options and work with the school and their children to assist appropriately.

COMMUNITY

Educators need to know what our students can accomplish, not what they should *not* try to accomplish. The community must understand and support school initiatives.

> "If a doctor, lawyer, or dentist had 30 people in his/her office at one time, all of whom had different needs, and some of whom didn't want to be there and, thus, were causing trouble and disruption . . . and if the doctor, lawyer, or dentist, without assistance, had to treat them all with professional dedication and excellence for nine straight months, then he/she might have some conception of the classroom teacher's job" (author unknown).

The community's support and understanding of change in education is crucial for support to come through boards of education and budget votes. People who live in a community but have no children from their homes attending school must be invited and welcomed participants in school activities.

Many activities can involve different members of the school community to foster a caring, sharing partnership between students, faculty, parents, and other community members.

School clubs can develop partnerships with senior citizens both in support of and to receive support from older members of the community. Senior citizens can be invited to school plays, sporting events, and activities such as blood drives. Seniors can be recipients of club gifts—student visits one hour per month for companionship or funds for a trip to visit family members during a holiday.

Dr. Hasna Muhammad, an assistant principal at the Monroe Woodbury Middle School in Central Valley, New York, created (with colleagues) the concept of a "garden of respect." Students who had negative interactions with adults or peers were scheduled to work in the garden as a way of understanding that there were alternative choices to replace negative behavior. Other community members supported the garden of respect by donating flowers, working with students in the garden, etc. Community builds communities of mutual respect by working together on a shared goal. This garden is a wonderful example of how to actualize this concept for all stakeholders.

Brotherhood
by Harold Heller

What is more important than the dignity of man?
Treating all his equals is the best way that one can
Elevate men's spirits, make them partners in our clan;
Brotherhood's the finest gift that man can give to man.

Nothing costs so little, yet can make one feel so great.
Spreading hope and comfort has a way to compensate
Those that love their fellow man no matter what his state;
Brotherhood's the key to open humanity's brightest gate.

4

Inclusion—The "I" Word

Inclusion is an often misused term, which creates reactions from parents, teachers, and administrators. Those who respond favorably typically believe that inclusion is a law and that all children can benefit from inclusion. People who react negatively often believe inclusion is a law with questionable definition and believe children with disabilities are "dumped" into school situations that do not take the needs of all students and staff into consideration. Neither assumption is correct.

The popularization of the word "inclusion" has brought about a significant reaction from both special educators and classroom educators. Between the late 1980s and early 1990s, the inclusion movement arrived on the doorstep of schools throughout the nation (Aefsky, 1995). Although the entitlement of LRE had been in effect since the inception of P.L. 92-147 (1975), this provision was highlighted after the Federal Government audited states, and discovered that the LRE requirement was not consistently followed, causing many disabled students to be placed in restrictive, separate instructional settings. The "I" word caused many educators to panic, falsely believing that all disabled children, regardless of individual needs, would be placed into an age appropriate classroom. This was *never* the intent. Some district leaders who believed this to be the case made errors in trying to stay ahead of perceived regulations, and teachers believed students were "dumped" into their classrooms without necessary support or logical information sharing. Needless to say, undoing errors caused distrust and disillusionment among teachers, administrators, parents, and students.

The lack of succinct, accurate information caused problems between teacher unions, administration, and parents. Media coverage exacerbated the situation. Because legislative involvement in special education enabled students with disabilities to receive a free, appropriate, public education, practitioners have been informed of many regulations through special-education administrators. These practitioners include hierarchical central office administration and members of boards of education. Federal mandates dictate state regulations, and the states inform LEA special-education administration of mandate and regulatory changes. If school organizations and individual school buildings are all involved with providing services to disabled children, the question regarding why important information is not provided as an integral communication to all building and district administrators is a valid one.

Twenty years after mandated compliance with LRE entitlements and concern about the lack of coordination between regular and special educators, communication is still separated between disciplines. Teachers, parents, and students are still fighting a battle of varied intensity to provide collaborative services to shared students, yet the communication system has not blended the building-level needs for teachers, administrators, or students. Inclusion does not have to be, nor should it be, a special education "movement." It is part of an educational focus on collaborative teaching for diverse student learners.

The National Middle School Association published a position paper in 1995, entitled "This We Believe." Its purpose was to serve as a guide to schools in providing developmentally responsive educational programs to young adolescents, grades 6–8. Goals suggested for responsible middle level education include:

- Educators committed to young adolescents
- Shared vision
- High expectations for all
- Positive school climate
- Challenging curriculum
- Varied teaching and learning approaches

- Flexible organizational structure
- Assessment and evaluation that promote learning

These are the *same* characteristics that are promoted for inclusive programs:

- A shared vision for teaching students, utilizing a variety of teaching and learning approaches that engage learners, provide hands-on experiences, and encourage cooperative learning groups
- Assessment (measuring student progress toward goals or objectives) and evaluation (using data and standards to judge quality of progress that promote learning) for providing feedback, and use in planning future endeavors to support student learning
- Flexible organizational structure in grouping, scheduling, and staffing; use of time, space, and staff
- Collaboration across teaching specialties; teachers share responsibility for curriculum and delivery of instruction

Identified problems of inclusion include:

- Lack of support (from administrators and colleagues)
- Lack of communication (among teachers, parents, and communities)
- No common planning time (daily, weekly, monthly)
- University preparation of teachers

Key Components for success of inclusion include:

- Focus on *students'* needs
- Teacher-directed, alternative teaching styles
- Administratively facilitated programs
- Communication between stakeholders
- Resource allocation
- Flexibility

ADMINISTRATIVE AND TEACHING CONSIDERATIONS

STRATEGIES THAT MAKE INCLUSION WORK

- Maintain continuum of services
- Retain special-education teaching space
- Reduction of special education support services
- Clustering students during scheduling process
- Shared planning time
- Heterogeneous groups for instruction
- Collaborative teaching
- Defined roles of special and regular (content) educators
- Curriculum adaptations
- Change in delivery of instruction
- Teaching assistants
- Staff development
- Parental support
- Communication

The concept of inclusion raised concern of educators in the areas of assessment, accountability, and resource support. Inclusion at the elementary-school level has been researched more than secondary-school inclusion, as there appears to be more inclusion in the lower grades. Baker and Zigmond (1995) compiled data from five school sites from the Southeast to the Northwest (Virginia, Pennsylvania, Kansas, Minnesota, and Washington). They acknowledged student and staff enthusiasm, but noted that faculty were asked to volunteer and questioned the message teachers were given. Inclusion is a result of LRE. If faculty choose *not* to be involved with students with disabilities, they will never attempt to understand or cooperate with inclusive programs.

Teachers should not have the luxury of choosing their students in special or regular education programs. They are paid to educate their assigned students, and when building administrators sort students by teacher choice, they create potential conflict, even if the original intent was to avoid conflict. If a school supports teacher choice of students, then who teaches the students no one chooses? This situation is reminiscent of team sports on the playground: the last one chosen feels badly, unwanted, and unsuccessful. Are these the feelings that educators want to encourage in children? I don't believe any educator wants any child to feel badly. However, when people choose to work in a comfortable environment with students whose needs they perceive as familiar, change is postponed and the status quo remains. Building leaders need to support people in change, so that the adults can feel positive and valued. They, in turn, will support the students in feeling positive about change, and encouraging student success.

Inclusive programs in elementary schools have been identified as more successful than secondary-school inclusive programs, based on content of elementary as compared to secondary program components. Ysseldyke (1997) discussed "lessons from a negative example of inclusion" in a middle school. He studied a Midwestern middle school, where teachers and students were organized into teams. Included students were clustered into one team at each grade level (6, 7, and 8). After one year of implementation, negative evaluations included the following:

- Inadequate ongoing training, communication, and planning
- Lack of responsibility of general educators for implementing program components
- Minimal support from the principal, who offered words, not actions
- Lack of willingness of classroom teachers to modify teaching styles
- Lack of special educators' confidence that regular teachers would keep included students in class and modify assignments, rather than separate students whenever an academic concern arose

However, positive attributes were identified, even though the article title led the reader to believe only negative results developed. These included:

- Attitudes of other students.
- Positive social development of all students in the class.
- Staff learned that students could be included without impeding other students and without chaos developing.

The author pointed out that change occurs over time, and schools need to focus on six main points:

- Building leaders need to be active supporters.
- Staff must know they can't choose students; they will have included students.
- Educating students is a *shared responsibility*.
- Involve parents.
- Establish a shared vision.
- Establish mechanisms to learn from the process as it evolves.

Successful Secondary Inclusion Models

Districts across the country have developed successful secondary inclusion models. A major difference between elementary and secondary programs lies in the content specificity that departmentalized secondary-school educators require. Secondary-level educators need to develop a way for content specialists to work with a team of special educators so that each special educator is not planning more that 2 content areas. (At the elementary level, teachers typically expect to teach all subject areas, so this issue is not as complex.) One way to accomplish a successful inclusion model is to have a team of six teachers—four subject teachers and two special educators, each covering two content classes. This team approach allows for content experts to work with one special education teacher, and the two

TABLE 4. A COMPARISON OF SPECIAL-EDUCATION SERVICES FOR SEIRC STUDENTS

	1992–1993 (fifth grade)	1996–1997 (ninth grade)
1.	FTS (full-time services)	SEIRC
2.	PTS (part-time services)	Declassified
3.	PTS	Skills only
4.	PTS	Skills only
5.	FTS	Skills only
6.	PTS	Declassified
7.	FTS	SEIRC
8.	PTS	SEIRC
9.	FTS	Skills only
10.	PTS	Declassified
11.	FTS	SEIRC
12.	PTS	Skills only
13.	PTS	SEIRC
14.	FTS	SEIRC
15.	FTS	SEIRC

Note: Declassified indicates that the student no longer receives special education support.

special education teachers can coordinate instruction and skill development between assigned students. The addition of special education teaching assistants or paraprofessionals allows for further teaming, and coordination of instruction for all students.

An example of a student-success driven inclusion model is in the Monroe-Woodbury Central School District (MWCSD), Central Valley, New York. The Special Education in the Regular Class (SEIRC) model began in a seventh-grade pilot program during the 1994–1995 school year, under the direction of Dr. Phil Paterno, Director of Pupil Personnel Services. The model expanded as students were promoted to higher grades. Table 4 demonstrates a key concept of a positive secondary inclusion program: students are successful with fewer special education services, as support provided in the regular class is sufficient for many students with mild to moderate disabilities, with one period of skills or resource room support each day.

One of the high school SEIRC teachers surveyed ninth-grade SEIRC students in June 1997. Students were asked to respond to the following question: "How is an SEIRC class different from a special education class for you?" Student responses are reported in Table 5.

A critical evaluation of program success was a measure of student progress and success. Many teachers expressed concern about expanding the SEIRC model, stating that special-education students would not get the help they needed, and that typical students would suffer the negative consequences of being in an inclusive setting. Middle-school and high-school data were reviewed and results are presented in Tables 6, 7, and 8 in Appendixes E and F.

As indicated by data presented, students who received support in the SEIRC model, disabled students mainstreamed for a subject, and regular-education students did not present with significantly different profiles, in terms of achievement levels, report-card grades, or IQ scores. It is a misconception that mildly to moderately disabled students are *very* different than non-disabled peers. In fact, there are more similarities than differences. Most disabled students are classified as learning disabled, which, by definition, indicates average or better intellectual capabilities. Other disability categories, such as emotionally disabled, other health impaired, orthopedically impaired, and hearing or visually impaired can be indicative of students with average or above average intelligence.

At the beginning of the second year of SEIRC at the Monroe-Woodbury High School, many non-disabled students who had been in collaboratively taught sections in ninth grade and were not in these sections in tenth grade, went to guidance asking for schedule changes. The students stated that they "did better" in classes when there were two teachers present. This occurrence lent itself to the belief that non-disabled students perceived SEIRC classes to be of benefit to them.

TABLE 5. NINTH GRADERS TELL HOW SEIRC CLASSES DIFFER FROM SEGREGATED CLASSES, JUNE 1997

Better kids, less distraction.

Teach faster here.

A normal class with a little help.

Special ed class makes you feel like you are stupid.

It's easier to work because you get more attention.

It makes you feel like you are getting somewhere.

I work harder to achieve what I want.

It is important to remind faculty involved with change that student data drive change, for if students cannot achieve desired outcomes, the student, teacher, principal, and district are held accountable. Encourage teachers to ask questions, and provide resources necessary to obtain answers requested.

In Monroe-Woodbury CSD, the success of the secondary SEIRC program expanded to lower and higher grades. During the 1997–1998 school year, the model was piloted at the fifth- and sixth-grade level at one of three elementary schools. In these models, a special education teacher, teaching assistant, and two classroom teachers team taught approximately 64 children. Previously all disabled students attended full-time, separate special-education classrooms, with varied levels of mainstreaming. The special-education teacher maintained a class space so that additional support could be provided for *any* member of the classes. During the year, flexibility was the key component to the students' and teachers' success. Challenges were encountered and dealt with by the team, with building- and district-level administrative support. Although each team functioned in its own way, as determined by teachers involved, the students' success led to the expansion of the pilot into the two other elementary schools at the sixth-grade level, and the fifth-grade level at one of the other elementary schools.

The success of SEIRC required balance between educators, psychologists, teachers (special and content), administrators, and parents to ensure that appropriate special education services were provided to eligible students, in the least restrictive setting. When students performed well with support, professionals and parents were fearful of taking support away, even if the students were no longer eligible for services. Communication between stakeholders and coordination of regular-education support available to non-disabled students (remediation) was a significant component of the school community.

The Monroe-Woodbury CSD moved to a 6–8 middle-school configuration and a new high school was occupied (September 1999), creating a domino effect of change in the district. Teachers were cautiously optimistic about all the changes that occurred, and inclusion expansion was an additional variable to contend with for some educators. The faculty's commitment to students prevailed, and programs moved forward to a shared vision, driven by student success. All but 3 of the 29 children in grades 5 and 6 during 1997–1998 continued in a SEIRC model for the 1998–1999 school year. If the pilot had not been attempted, it is likely that all but three students would be in more restrictive settings. In fact, students in a class with an inclusive component have demonstrated positive total class success as measured by state and district testing.

In many districts, inclusion by opportunity is encouraged by teachers and administration and welcomed by parents. In the SEIRC models mentioned above, each student's IEP states that services will be provided for students with supplemental support and service in the regular class, as determined by the eligibility committee. For students receiving service in part-time, pull-out models, principals have clustered disabled students, rather than distribute a few per class, so that teachers can choose to collaborate on how children can meet IEP goals and objectives. At times, students remain in their class and the special education teacher works in the regular classroom, and at other times, students are pulled out for service delivery. When students are clustered, options exist.

Districts that cluster mild to moderately disabled students have found that teachers attempt to utilize more collaborative practices and decide to work with colleagues on behalf of all students. Caution must be noted, because it is easy for special educators to want to expand options, when the number of assigned students might not allow for expansion without added staff. Inclusion is not automatically more or less costly, and both building-level and district administration must monitor and adjust schedules so that the needs of all students and faculty are met within reasonably set parameters. Once this information is obtained for students, clustering by area(s) of need will allow for inclusion by opportunity, and teachers can focus on subject-area determination of support for students.

A GUIDE TO SPECIAL EDUCATION IN THE REGULAR CLASS (SEIRC)

Basic Philosophy

- Mild to moderately disabled students
- Individually determined, under LRE guidelines
- Cost cannot be excessive (should be at or near cost as pull-out programs with rearranged resources)

Elementary level

- Need to cluster five to eight students in regular class
- Skills or resource room period each day
- Teachers need to team-teach
- Building principal needs to arrange for shared planning time for teacher collaboration
- Staff development workshops need to be provided for staff
- Planned communication between administrators and teachers, teacher and teacher, and teachers and parents

- System in place for revisions, flexibility, encourage risk-taking on behalf of student success

Secondary level (additional considerations)

- Scheduling options within departmentalized building schedule (content and flexibility focus)
- High expectations and changing standards require support by provision of resources for positive student achievement

Building leaders can facilitate successful outcomes for all students by planning creative course opportunities and structures with faculty members. New standards K–12, resulting in higher expectations for students meeting necessary high school graduation requirements have been implemented by each state on a national level. This change has resulted in the need for district wide revisions across curricular areas in all grades.

Building administrators can supervise the development of course and curricular changes that assist all learners by sharing resources in a different manner. For example, one approach is pooling staff members who taught supplemental content in support programs (i.e. remedial support, developmental courses, or subject area learning labs). Clustering students who need specific types of support enable the building leader to schedule team-taught periods.

Content classes can be developed to support needs of students. For example, a reading/writing or literacy course can be developed for students with poor reading/writing skills in grades 7–12 (typically, English or language arts replaces a separate reading class at these levels).

Course content should be derived from a task analysis of the scope and sequence of skills required for high school graduation in English, and this extra class for identified students would focus on additional time on those skills.

Students would receive course credit, and would benefit from additional periods over a multi-year time span, in weak areas of basic skills.

FIGURE 1

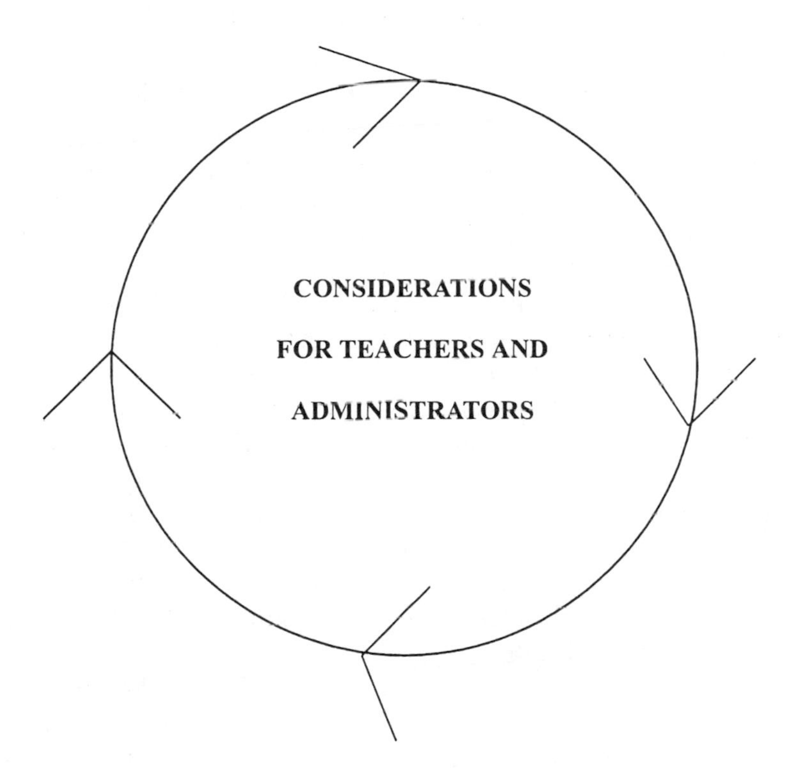

1) How students learn

2) How we teach

3) Strengths

4) Weaknesses

5) Modalities

6) Environment

7) Strategies

8) Reactions

THE STUDENTS—OUR FOCUS

STUDENTS

Schools exist for children, because without students, there would be no need for schools. Therefore, the needs of students must always come first in developing programs. The needs of staff members follow so that they can ensure student needs are met. All students are not the same, which make educators' jobs interesting and different each day. However, all students are entitled to an education, so understanding different options for all students is relevant. Some students are "at-risk" for difficulties in school, and are not classified as disabled. Some disabled students are not identified as problems in educational settings. Some students (both disabled and non-disabled) are identified as having significant behavioral problems.

Children of all ages need to feel that they are respected members of the class and school. Students need to feel supported in the learning environment. Teachers need to recognize the different needs of students and their own teaching style. Decision making on behalf of student need might require altering teaching styles so that students can demonstrate knowledge.

Children in elementary schools want to please adults, and they often are able to do just that. Adolescents are viewed as "older" by many adults, and are "supposed" to be able to understand and comply with school rules. However, educators need to remind themselves that developmental stages are just as applicable to 15-year-olds as they are to 6-year-olds. Developmentally, adolescents are supposed to challenge authority and test limits. Behaviors that demonstrate these characteristics are *typical* adolescent behaviors. It is *our* responsibility as educators to understand this, and allow students to make appropriate choices with appropriate guidance from us. Adolescents might not comply with authority at all times, but if the authority understands developmental stages, and acts fairly, students will respect the adult, even if they choose not to comply with the adult.

Building leaders have to demonstrate a high level of understanding and support for students so educators have positive options that support students. If an administrative "solution" is to suspend or "get rid" of a student, teachers simply learn to follow that lead. As a result, we as a society lose the respect of a child and we contribute to feelings of anger and uselessness. That *is not* why educators become educators. Our job is to *help* children, and there are ways we can help even those who make poor choices. We *cannot* help them if we "get rid" of them.

Decisions that are student-centered can help children of all ages learn to make better choices. These decisions demonstrate that adults care about them as young adults. Educators can support and demonstrate to children that all children in their school are important members of the school society.

5

STAFF DEVELOPMENT

The purpose of staff development programs is to support school staff members and refine their continuing knowledge about the way children learn. Staff development programs must help teachers refine what they teach and help them implement techniques and strategies that enhance student learning. Professional development activities should be an integral part of every professional's continuing education plan.

District and building administrators need to support staff-development workshops for paraprofessionals, teachers, and administrators who work with diverse learners. The development of district-wide initiatives for collaboration between disciplines encourages teachers to develop a positive mindset regarding the way they instruct and support shared students. Special education and classroom teachers at all levels and in all disciplines benefit from professional growth and collaboration. When teachers have opportunities to work with colleagues, they facilitate professional growth activities by maximizing each other's areas of strength. Furthermore, their expertise becomes known among colleagues. If the school and district environment encourages and plans for these opportunities for faculty, everyone benefits—the organization, the administration, the faculty, and the students.

Most districts plan a few days each year for teacher in-service workshops. Each year, a day-long, district-wide workshop should be dedicated to inclusion. Separate workshops should be developed for elementary- and secondary-school teachers. The misconceptions about inclusion are great. When a district focuses a workshop for *all* faculty on this issue, individuals who make up schools and the educational organization learn to value the importance and positive benefits of inclusion. Input from staff should be gathered and data from students should be shared. Earlier in this book, I mentioned Fullan's (1996) view of the importance of teacher input. Teachers who believe that the school organization wants and processes their input value the school culture and system. Sparks and Loucks (1989) identified six elements of effective staff development:

- Links to school-wide initiatives
- In-service workshops planned by teachers
- Differentiated training opportunities
- Teacher-selected goals and activities
- Concrete training that is supported over time and that includes demonstration, supervised trials, and feedback
- Ongoing assistance and support (resources of time and money)

These six elements support the concepts of team teaching and collaboration of educators. Again, inclusion is not a separate entity from other educational reform concepts. In fact, it is very similar to most.

Teachers' and administrators' difficulty with the concepts of change, team teaching, and collaboration must be acknowledged and addressed. Educational leaders must then plan and organize systemic change. Teachers often view change as a "passing fancy," based on previous experiences with *curricular* debates (whole-language versus phonics; drill-and-skill math versus conceptual programs; self-contained classes versus inclusion services for students with disabilities) and management/leadership styles (top-down versus bottom-up, site-based management and shared decision making versus centralized command and control). Evaluation procedures often inhibit innovation and risk-taking, because teachers might perceive that supervisors are looking for guaranteed success and order in an observed lesson.

Practitioners know that educating children is an exciting

opportunity and find joy in observing children gain knowledge. Obstacles can seem overwhelming, but collegial support and administrative leadership provide structure for group problem solving and creative solutions that benefit students, staff, and parents. Education is a complex balance between parallel universes of psychological (how children learn) and educational (what is deemed valuable for students to know) interactions between children, educators, school environments and community cultures. Learning organizations are where people continually learn to learn together (Senge, 1990).

Organizational change needs structure, support, communication, and mutual adaptation. Rogers (1962) identified four stages of the change processes. Early adopters jump on the bandwagon at the outset, and represent 7–10 percent of the targeted population. Latent adopters follow others and represent 25–35 percent of the targeted population. Laggards follow when necessary for survival; they constitute 35–45 percent of the population targeted for change. Resisters (7–10 percent) are impossible to convince and must be directed by supervisors to do their job. At an educators' workshop where this concept was presented by Dr. Bruce McKenna (July, 1998), participants agreed that these concepts agreed with observed behaviors in themselves or colleagues regarding the delivery of special education services to students in shared learning environments. Student and teacher grade level did not seem to impact the attitudes or feelings of the audience. Recognizing that change is a process in which individuals and then organizations make change is critical to the health of any organization.

Staff input, reaction, and concerns must be requested and addressed. Building administrators must reinforce the concepts of legal compliance and student achievement as *goals* of the school for students with disabilities. If educational leaders talk about all students as ours (not yours and mine), staff will follow and be proactive, collaborative problem solvers. Modeling positive behavior impacts school climate positively. If we learn to teach differently, we learn to teach the love of learning to students who learn differently.

High-stakes exams, which assess levels of the "new standards" of student achievement, are a focus of every educational community. Resources for central administrators, principals, teachers (both special and content educators) at K–12 levels, parents and students need to be available in each local district and building library. Educators need time to look at available resources, supported by district administration and board of education members. For example, a new teacher might not know the people who are required to attend an eligibility meeting. Teacher resource guides should be available for an explanation of the eligibility process in *each* district. State guides serve a general purpose of explaining the special education process, but variations of eligibility meetings exist in each district. The information a teacher gathers about the process prior to attending a meeting assists all stakeholders. Parental discussions can take place regarding projected recommendations and questions can be addressed to special and content teachers prior to the meeting.

The resource of *time* is one that educators continually identify as a need. Building-level and district administrators should try to collaboratively seek district support for teachers to spend in-service workshop days on self-directed, student-support activities. Teachers want to succeed, and want their students to succeed. We need to refocus energies on providing local support for teacher-to-teacher conferences at the local level.

Staff-development training workshops need to focus on the characteristics of adult learning. Adults learn through the following:

- Modeling
- Doing
- Practicing
- Refining
- Reflecting
- Evaluating
- Communicating

If training teaches staff members how to learn new techniques, it is highly likely that those techniques will be transferred into classroom instruction and practice. For example, if staff have fun with an activity presented, they will see how students can have fun as well. Additionally, staff members will assume they have administrative permission to try new techniques in their classroom to encourage student learning and success.

A district's teacher-evaluation process should further encourage and reinforce innovative practice. If a checklist is used for establishing teacher goals and objectives for the school year, a section on creativity and innovation for delivery of instruction strongly supports teachers' willingness to try new ideas. Teachers often fear creativity because they feel that administrators and colleagues will question their ability, especially if an activity is unsuccessful. Parents and educators encourage students to learn from mistakes and move forward. This same philosophy should be utilized to encourage teachers to be motivated instructors for students of all ages and abilities. A district's teacher-evaluation process should further encourage and reinforce innovative practice. If a checklist is used for establishing teacher goals and objectives for the school year, a section on creativity and innovation for delivery of instruction strongly supports teachers' willingness to try new ideas.

STAFF-DEVELOPMENT ACTIVITIES

The following activities can be used in staff training as models for activities staff members can use with students. Each activity can be modified for elementary and secondary educators and students, using a little imagination and creative thinking. These examples include information about how each activity can be used with curriculum content and standards, collaborative grouping and teaming for classroom tasks, and student management, using alternative teaching strategies for large and small groups of students.

ACTIVITY 1. ESTABLISHING A SHARED VISION

FACULTY

Building leaders can use the following exercise at a faculty or grade-level meeting. For the past four years, I have had the opportunity to present workshops on inclusion in various states, overseas, and in graduate-level classes. Results of this activity have been the same as those reported below.

Arrange the members of the meeting into groups of four. Hand out page 123, and then ask the groups to collaboratively list three to five thoughts on each topic.

Then facilitate a discussion of responses. Post them on the board. Then distribute page 124 and ask groups to identify similarities.

In all workshop and class activities, the similarities exposed in this activity astounded many, helping teachers and administrators realize that inclusive practice and reform are part of and synonymous with other educational reform and restructuring efforts.

Similar activities can be created to facilitate analytical activities for students. Children of various ages can be told by a teacher to think about a concept in a particular way, then be given an activity sheet to complete, where a different concept is actually being described. Students can then compare, debate or describe similarities and differences. For example, a culture in a social studies area can be the basis of a worksheet, and students can be asked to complete the answers based on their own experience. The teacher can then show an overhead of the culture being studied. Students can compare their responses to that of the ancient or foreign culture. When student-driven activities are connected to real life, student interest, motivation, and retention of information are increased. Constructivists suggested that meaningful learning occurs within an individual's logical framework, created by environment and experience (Fosnot, 1989). Jensen (1998) stated that building connections for students in the classroom assists students in developing memory. The brain develops patterns, which enable better recall and retention. Acronyms and mnemonics are useful tools because the synapse connections and pattern the brain creates allow for associations to trigger responses.

STUDENTS

This activity can be modified for classroom use for discussing or researching cultural differences and historical events. The

Planning Inclusive Classrooms

Shared vision

Goals

Desired learning outcomes

Standards

A framework for curriculum and assessment

Standards for professional practice

Organizational structures

Elements of the Educational Blueprint: Education 2000

Shared vision: The foundation of the blueprint is the community's vision of schools and schooling for the 21st Century.

Goals: Represent the community's educational values, and answer the question "prepared for what?"

Desired learning outcomes: Derived from and form the goals; the desired measurable or observable outcomes of what students should know.

Standards: The levels, types of knowledge, and performance expected of students.

Framework for curriculum and assessment: Guides the development of curriculum and ensures that all students have the opportunity to achieve the outcomes, divided into three parts:

> **Curriculum strands:** Give direction to what is taught
>
> **Benchmarks:** Set target for measuring student progress toward meeting the standards.
>
> **Assessment and curriculum strategies:** Tie together strands and benchmarks.

Standards for professional practice: Best of what we know about effective teaching, and integrated into a belief system for the entire school community (teachers, administrators, support staff)

Organizational structures: Facilitation of an organizational plan for decision making, communication, and allocation of resources, in order to help students reach desired outcomes.

(Kniep, 1995)

activity can be used in other creative ways to learn about content, social, and behavioral concepts. Teachers can plan small-group activities of filling in the outline given, and having students brainstorm ideas. The teacher can then facilitate a discussion of comparison.

ACTIVITY 2. HOOK PROJECT

FACULTY

Pass out pictures of a hook on 8 1/2 x 11 sheets of paper (*see* Appendix G), and writing or drawing instruments of at least two colors. Ask participants to draw a picture in two minutes. When time is up, sort the group by attributes of the picture drawn (ask people to move to corners of the room). Sort by vertical versus horizontal pictures, end results (balloon, lollipops, suns, etc.), until there are at least four different groups sorted by similarity of drawing. Name each group, where one name sounds better than the others. Go around to the groups and talk about their pictures. For the next few minutes, use inflection in your voice to positively support the "favored" group, making satisfactory comments about the other three groups, but with noted difference when talking about the pictures in the "favored" group. Ask adults to write a group response to what they thought of this activity. The "favored" group will write the most positive statements, reflecting how they as learners were treated.

Use the results to show teachers how their words and actions in a classroom set a tone for student motivation and response, without intending to treat students differently. Discuss the importance of creating a positive classroom environment where all students can participate without fear of feeling different in a negative way than peers.

STUDENTS

Classroom teachers who have diverse student populations can benefit from this activity. Teachers can demonstrate how different groups of students (high and low achievers, rich and poor, bullies, differences in ethnicity or religion, students with disabilities, etc.) feel when treated by others, positively and negatively. Have participants draw a picture from the hook, and write a sentence or two describing their pictures. When students are done, commend those students who are not used to being the "better students." Commend them on colors used, content of drawing, or any positive attribute. This will enable students who typically struggle with handwriting, written expression, and school tasks to have their moment to shine among peers and feel successful and worthy as learners. What a motivating day it will be!

ACTIVITY 3. CREATING A SOCIAL HIERARCHY

FACULTY

Sort people by the color shirt they are wearing or by the color of their eyes. People with green eyes may not be allowed to speak to anyone other than another person with green eyes. Establish that the green-eyed participants form group 1, blue-eyed participants form group 2, and so on. A group treasure hunt is then initiated, where each group needs another group for one or more of the steps to complete the activity. Typically, the "favored" group needs no one else, and the "lowest group" needs a lot of support. Structure this activity so that the groups know their standing after the sorting part of the activity, and then reverse the order for the activity completion ("lowest group" needs no one, "favored group" needs help from everyone).

Presenting opportunities for staff to know what it *feels* like to be in the "high" or "low" group is a powerful tool to use. The "affective side of learning is the critical interplay between how we feel, act, and think" (Jensen, 1998, p. 71). Emotions play an important role in our ability to teach and be attentive to diverse needs of students.

STUDENTS

This sorting activity can be used when studying the Holocaust, Civil Rights, the Roman Empire, ancient Egypt, or other historical events. Plan how to establish groups, establish a "favored" and "lowest group" and then reverse expectations in a student activity.

Presenting opportunities so students know what it *feels* like to be involved during the presenting problem is a powerful tool to use. Students will relate to the topic better when it is connected to their real world of events. This will enable students to learn, remember, and recall facts in an enhanced manner.

ACTIVITY 4. SETTING THE TONE OF THE LEARNING ENVIRONMENT

FACULTY

Use a staff conference day to schedule a learning-center activity for staff. In each learning center (different classrooms) have music playing that "sets the tone" for the activity. Play a relaxing tape for staff to develop a lesson plan. Have loud music playing for a physical activity, and have classical music playing for a third directed activity for one group of staff. Then do the same activities with a second group of staff members, but *rotate* the music type played. Position an observer in each session to compare speed of completion of activities between the two groups.

STUDENTS

Playing different types of music in a classroom can set different tones for students. If music is quiet, it can have a calming effect on the environment. Fast music compels listeners to complete something quickly. Music can set the pace for certain classroom activities. If music is played during the first five minutes of a class when students write in their journal, you may see a difference based on the background music speed and intensity. Try this for a week or two, and keep track of the type of music played during journal writing. You will discover an interesting pattern of students' writing and find this strategy can be used in other instructional activities.

Younger children can complete fine and gross motor tasks with music tempo and older children can read with soft music in the background. Students can compete with music as a timer (e.g., the music played while contestants are answering Jeopardy's final question). Gardner's (1993) description of multiple intelligences suggested ways to enhance learning by recognizing the different attributes of learning students possess. Varying teaching strategies so that all modalities are involved will enable all students to gain knowledge. Again, using assorted techniques and strategies to help students succeed requires the ability of teachers to implement innovative lessons. Staff evaluation practice and educational leaders must support these initiatives.

ACTIVITY 5. BEACH BALL TOSS

FACULTY

At the end of a faculty presentation, divide the staff into small groups. Give each group a beach ball and a black marker. Ask each group to blow up its beach ball, and fill in each section with a word or phrase that sums up an important concept discussed. When all groups have filled each slot with at least one word or phrase, have the groups switch balls, and play the following game. Pass or toss the ball around, and wherever a thumb lands when a person catches the ball, the word or phrase is read and reacted to by the group. Observe how much fun the group has as they determine how they use the beach ball and how they review the content of the presentation.

STUDENTS

This activity is a fun way to reinforce, practice, and review vocabulary and concepts in content areas. Teachers can create a sample by using a marker to write a word or concept in each colored section of a beach ball. Students then pass or toss the ball around, and wherever their thumb lands when they catch the ball determines what response is required. If a student does not know the correct response, they toss it to a peer for assistance. This can be a five- to ten-minute activity, engaging students in a stimulating manner. Movement is a wonderful way to stimulate interest.

Educational games that include movement enable children to focus energy on tasks rather than "fidget in their seats." Think of adults at a training seminar or at work. There are breaks every hour or so. People take walks, swim, and jog during their lunch hours. Exercising your body also exercises your mind. The same is true for students. Alternating thinking and doing during a class period encourages activity of the mind with the presented task. Children who are required to sit and complete worksheets for long periods in class are not able to demonstrate knowledge. Boredom develops, and as a result, a teacher may spend more time repeating content that students have not bothered to learn. Change the environment for learning, and watch sparks of interest ignite.

ACTIVITY 6. COLOR-CODING

FACULTY

Bring in five different items of five different colors (paper clips, Post-It Notes or Tabs, bubble gum, or plastic beads). Give groups of participants six of each item, and blank index cards. Ask staff to create a lesson using only these materials to plan a multiplication, division, addition, or subtraction lesson. The group then writes up the lesson, and presents it to the larger group. Teachers can then adapt a similar activity for students to use in the classroom.

STUDENTS

This version of the color coding activity pertains to research in a topic area. Take a unit or theme. Have groups of students use Post-It Tabs to sort content from 3–5 different resources. Each group then shares information by color, so that each group is using peers' input for one color concept. Each group then develops a study guide in outline form and shares the product with all other groups. This activity can occur over a short or long period of time, encouraging peer collaboration on varying levels.

Color-coding can be used to create a variety of interactive lessons at the elementary and secondary levels. Having students think of ways to color-code activities is an engaging activity for all learners.

RESOURCE SHARING

This section contains samples of resources for teachers and administrators. They are organized by elementary and secondary levels and may be copied and used for educational purposes by any reader of this book, as "educated bookshelves and file cabinets" are a useless resource. I hope that some of the activities and forms presented assist teachers and principals. A list of additional suggested readings for practitioners is included in chapter 6 and organized by topic.

FORMS FOR ELIGIBILITY MEETINGS

Classroom and special education teachers need to submit information about student progress for eligibility meetings. The information the committee requires includes the following:

- Current academic needs and progress (including report cards, progress reports, earned credits)
- Description of social and emotional needs and progress
- Identification of behavioral and management needs and progress
- List of physical needs and progress

Goals and objectives on the IEP should be updated as often as report cards are sent home in the school (new IDEA 1997 requirement). The data should also be presented at eligibility and IEP meetings consistently.

An example of "Teacher Report to the Eligibility Committee" shows a delineation of progress in each subject area. The following form was developed for special education teachers of elementary students:

Teacher Report to Eligibility Committee: Elementary

Student Name ______________________________

Teacher ________________________ Date ________

Describe strengths and weaknesses in each subject area:

Reading:

Math:

Science:

Social Studies:

Behavioral and social interaction:

Other:

Comments:

Teacher Report to Eligibility Committee: Secondary

Student Name ______________________________

Teacher ______________________ Date ________

Describe strengths and weaknesses in each subject area:

Math:

Science:

History:

English:

Electives:
1.

2.

3.

4.

Comments

Teacher Report to the Eligibility Committee

Student ____________________ Teacher ________________

Date ________ Grade __________ DOB _________

Subject ________________________

Please list student needs and progress in each area.

Describe current academic needs and progress (include report-card grades, individual achievement scores, curriculum-based assessment(s), and the samples from student's portfolio, if appropriate):

Please describe current social and emotional needs and progress:

Describe management and behavioral needs and progress:
List any physical, medical needs or concerns:

Elementary IEP Goals Update Report

Student ______________________ DOB ________

Date ___________ Teacher ___________________

School _____________________ Grade _________

Reading:

Math:

Science:

Social Studies:

Behavioral and social interaction:

Other:

Comments:

Secondary IEP Goals Update Report

Student ______________________ DOB ________

Date ___________ Teacher ____________________

School _____________________ Grade _________

Math:

Science:

History:

English:

Electives:
1.

2.

3.

4.

Comments:

One example of how special education teachers can effectively *communicate* with other teachers seen by their students is to implement a contact log. This log enables the teacher to quickly check-off contact achieved or needed. An example of a form some special education teachers use for this purpose follows:

Special Education Teacher Contact Log

Student Name ______________________________

Month S O N D J F M A M J

(Circle and color-code months)

(5 months per sheet; 2 sheets per child per year.)

Subject ____________________ Teacher ________________

Comments

Comments

Comments

Comments

Comments

The purpose of an instructional modification form is to identify data from a student's IEP that content teachers need to have on file in order to implement IEP modifications appropriately. These forms can provide a quick resource to educators who work with disabled students.

Instructional Modification Form

Student Name ____________________ DOB ___________

Grade _________ Disabling condition ________________

Medical alerts ________________ Medication _________

Strengths:
____ Reading ____ Language Arts ____ Math ____
____ Social Studies ____ Science

Comments:

Weaknesses:
____ Reading ____ Language Arts ____ Math
____ Social Studies ____ Science

Comments:

Learning modality:
____ Auditory ____ Visual ____ Tactile ____ Multisensory

Behavioral Concerns:
____ None ____ Minimal ____ Some concern
____ Functional behavioral plan in place (see attached)

Comments:

Instructional Modification Form

Student Name ____________________ DOB __________

Grade ________ Disabling condition __________________

Test modifications:

____ Tests read ____ Directions read ____ Extended time

____ Excused from grammar, spelling, and punctuation

____ Separate location ____ Alternate test format

____ Calculator ____ Answers recorded or scribed

____ Other ______________________________________

Student learns best when material is:

____ Auditorily presented

____ Visually presented

____ Study guide or outline presented for lecture

____ Presented with vocabulary before lessons

Behavior plan

____ Is not part of IEP

____ Is part of IEP

____ Components of plan attached

Student Data Sheet

Student Name ____________________ DOB ___________

Special Education teacher ___________________________

Strengths:

Weaknesses:

Test modifications:

____ Time limit waived or extended

____ Exam administered in separate location

____ Use of calculator

____ Large-print exams

____ Questions read

____ Modify method of response

____ Directions read

____ Other:

____

Behavior plan ____ yes ____ no

Teacher Input Form

Student Name ____________ DOB ______ Grade_____

Subject ____________________ Completed by _________

Behavior

Peer relationships:
_____ Excellent _____ good _____ fair _____ poor

Teacher relationships:
_____ Excellent _____ good _____ fair _____ poor

Group participation:
_____ Excellent _____ good _____ fair _____ poor

Demeanor of child:
_____ Active _____ shy _____ quiet _____other

Classroom performance

Academic level:

Strengths:

Weaknesses:

Attendance record:

What helps student succeed?

Checklist for Modifications

Student ______________________ Date ____________

Teacher ________________ School ________________

Strengths

____ Visual ____ Kinesthetic
____ Auditory ____ Multisensory
____ Tactile

Weaknesses

____ Visual ____ Kinesthetic
____ Auditory ____ Multisensory
____ Tactile

Testing Modifications

____ Tests read ____ Alternative location
____ Directions read ____ Oral response
____ Extended time ____ Answers scribed
____ Excused from grammar ____ Excused from punctuation
____ Reduce number of items per page
____ Use of aids:

Use the next page to assist teachers and parents in identifying strengths of children who learn best with a particular modality. Adaptation to curricular goals can be used to guide planning, ideas, and focus on learning strengths with alternative versions of this form.

Learning Style Checklist

Visual learners do:

1.

2.

3.

4.

5.

Auditory learners do:

1.

2.

3.

4.

5.

Tactile learners do:

1.

2.

3.

4.

5.

Multisensory learners do:

1.

2.

3.

4.

5.

TEACHING STRATEGIES FOR PREFERRED LEARNING MODALITIES

Visual Modality

Have students use:

- Bulletin boards
- Posters
- Transparencies
- Films
- VCR
- Blackboard
- Computers

Have students observe:

- Demonstrations
- Plays
- Experiments

Have students read:

- Books
- Maps
- Peers' notes

Provide students with:

- Outlines
- Study Guides
- Highlighted text
- Answer keys

Auditory Modality

Have students listen to:

- Books on tape
- Interviews

- Discussions
- Television
- Speeches
- Concerts
- Oral reports
- Brainstorming sessions

Tactile-Kinesthetic Modality

Have students touch:

- Objects
- Textures
- Weights

Have students:

- Write letters in sand
- Draw pictures
- Develop charts and graphs
- Construct models
- Paint
- Keep journals
- Create movies
- Finger-paint
- Play games
- Use manipulatives
- Complete experiments
- Act out literature/historical events

Multisensory Modality

Have students:

- Use more than one modality for each activity presented
- Enjoy exploration with activities

- Reinforce concepts with visual, auditory, and tactile-kinesthetic clues
- Use the body to integrate knowledge (hear it, say it, write it)

The worksheet on page 146 will help principals plan grouping for class placement. It will help plan clustering of students in a grade by similarity of IEP directed student need.

On page 147, you'll find the "Grading Modification Form." It is completed by the eligibility committee after it determines that a student's need, based on the nature and severity of his/her disability, entitles the student to modifications in grading. The completed form then becomes part of the student's IEP.

Worksheet for Clustering Students Based on Student Need

Classroom teacher______________________________

Special Education teacher ________________________

Grade _______ Total number of assigned students _____

Number of special education students ______________

Special education service checklist:
(Special education services based on student's IEP.)

(*Primary* indicates special education teacher teaches content. *Supportive* indicates extra help by special education teacher, but classroom teacher instructs child in subject.)

Reading
__ Primary __ Supportive

Language arts and writing
__ Primary __ Supportive

Math
__ Primary __ Supportive

Social Studies
__ Primary __ Supportive

Science
__ Primary __ Supportive

Study and organizational skills:

Management needs:

Grading Modification Form

Student name ________________________ Date _________

Special Education teacher _____________________________

Due to the nature and severity of this student's disability, the following modifications were recommended by the eligibility committee:

Report card grades in ______________________(subject(s)) should be calculated using the following percentage ranges:

Area	**Modified** (*circle one*)	**Percentage range**
Homework:	yes/no	___________
Tests:	yes/no	___________
Quizzes:	yes/no	___________
Projects:	yes/no	___________
Class participation:	yes/no	___________

Assignment modification to include:
____ multiple choice response
____ extended time
____ length of assignment shortened
____ provide study guide
____ notes provided
____ tape record lecture

Other:

Different

Ideas and

Variety between

Each other

Respect

Someone's

Individual abilities

Take the time to make

You and me = us

6

A Positive School Experience for All: Students, Faculty, Parents, and Community

Concepts of progressive leadership in schools depend on empowering people, so that they take ownership and personal interest in improving the classroom and school environment. Ongoing improvements are required as students, curriculum, and standards change. The best way to have support for a continuous cycle of improvement is by empowering all stakeholders (Byham, 1988).

Promoting and empowering teachers is an important concept for building leaders. When staff feels responsibility and identity with a concept of change, energy and power result (Byham, 1988). Innovation in schools requires a consistent program of district-wide professional training, public relations programs to build community support, resources of time and money, and a *commitment* of educational leaders to facilitate and support initiatives in their buildings, across disciplines, curriculum areas, student assessment and staff evaluation practices. Creating a network of "experts" within the school and district enables faculty members to "buy into" initiatives because they deem the initiatives worthy of the organization. The process of change, therefore, is recognized and valued.

Once goals and visions for change are *collaboratively* developed, based on any given framework for change, educators' *knowledge* is:

- Shared
- Defined
- Refined

- Implemented
- Practiced
- Evaluated
- Modified
- Repeated

Teachers often recognize these steps as necessary for their students' learning, but not for their own participation in changing curriculum, standards, and assessment practices. Educational leaders need to be able to assure teachers that the most important places in schools are their *classrooms*. Teachers must feel they have the support of administration and district resources to attend and provide training workshops for and with colleagues, be evaluated with a system that is compatible with teaching expectations of innovation and risk-taking. Teachers must feel able to ask questions and share comments without negative feedback.

As building and district leaders, educators need to remember that obstacles of emotional reaction to change must be overcome to achieve success. Past experience and failed expectations create negative reactions to a "new and wonderful" curriculum, teaching strategy, methodology, or assessment. All educators can recall instances when a "new" concept resulted in attending training workshops, buying new materials, and learning new instructional approaches. Later the "new" approach fell short based on changing philosophies, money dilemmas, or new administration at building or district level.

Publishers support "revised" materials due to the business aspect of supply and demand, and different publishers offer similar materials. The need to maintain competition and profit opposes the concept of long-term change.

Universities and colleges throughout the world support and demand research and publication from their professional staff members. Research typically occurs over a period of time (3–10+ years) and writing of results can occur two to three years after the end of gathering research data.

Why do K–12 educational systems change focus of curriculum, instructional philosophies and practice after only two to three years? Practitioners get frustrated when asked to participate in continually changing endeavors. Trust and competency are not developed, in either administration or concept material, on a personal or organizational level.

Districts and schools that review programs, policies, and curriculum on an ongoing cycle, and plan initiatives over a three to ten year cycle encourage trust and support of staff members. However, feedback from staff must be part of a consistent review component in order to further build trust of educators. When adults within an organization are valued, they often volunteer to facilitate future projects. Building a team within a school and the community encourages other members to participate in activities of school reform.

The principal's role is one that requires a commitment to the needs of the students, staff and community. Leadership requires coordination of tasks, feelings, expectations, standards, and assessment (Sergiovanni, 1992). Creating a caring learning environment supports all institutional and personal goals. A positive school climate encourages motivated learners, both adult and student.

The Five Ms of Leadership (Aefsky, 2000)

A building leader can create a positive school by implementing the five Ms of leadership:

- Maintaining a peaceful environment
- Motivating adult learners
- Managing details
- Modeling practices
- Maximizing staff potential

Maintaining a Peaceful Environment

Principals need to establish the right of school staff to agree or disagree with other professionals, parents, students, and administration. Communicating is the key as discussions and opinions should be expressed. This, of course, does not mean that decisions cannot be made by the principal, but it does support collaborative efforts supported by shared decision making initiatives. A caring environment facilitates innovation in practice.

MOTIVATING ADULT LEARNERS

Adults learners need different support as discussed in chapter 3. A building leader can motivate staff members by asking them to present ideas at various conferences and workshops. Another way to motivate staff is to have them write about a successful program for submission to a publication or teaching a course for colleagues. Having a professional "mini-organization" in the school where journal articles and books are shared and discussed is another concept supporting adult learning.

MANAGING DETAILS

Principals need to support staff in the everyday tasks of running a school building. Purchasing supplies, ordering books, working out scheduling conflicts, attending parent conferences, dealing with complaints, handling discipline, arranging field trips, and academic and sport competitions are activities teachers participate in on a daily basis. Building leaders who show support for teachers beyond classroom evaluations provide a significant measure of comfort for teachers.

MODELING PRACTICES

Principals set examples for staff members by what they do and discuss with staff. If principals limit themselves to what they already know and do not gain new knowledge, why should teachers? When a principal shares information gained through reading new books and articles, workshops attended, classes, and presentations, teachers value and share enthusiasm for new knowledge. This information often reinforces practitioners' instructional techniques and beliefs.

MAXIMIZING STAFF POTENTIAL

Teachers prioritize classroom tasks, because accountability for students and teachers is based on classroom activities. Principals can encourage staff members by acknowledging success on different levels, not only by standardized achievement results. Just as we ask teachers to communicate positive things to children and parents, we need to do the same with faculty members.

Lortie (1975) stated that "responsibility for the performance of peers will . . . be more readily accepted where teachers work together in highly integrated teams" (p. 238). In 1999, schools are organized with team teaching, looping, cooperative learning, block schedules, cross-curricular teams (math, science, and technology; math, science, social studies and English), peer tutoring, and mentoring programs. Both staff and student projects are team efforts.

FUTURE CONSIDERATIONS

Why are we still struggling as educational leaders with concepts addressed over 20 years ago? The cycle of change occurs, but what do we learn, what do we practice, and internalize?

Schools reflect society. As our society demands different attributes of school, school leaders facilitate change. The Dimensions of Learning/Teaching (Marzano, 1992) suggested that concepts are a general way of thinking. Educators are experts at conceptual change. Pragmatic change is difficult to achieve. The cycle of change must have purpose and be student focused and staff supported.

Concepts presented in this book apply to issues in special education, but can be utilized throughout educational systems. The concepts of P.L.94-142, in 1975 are not drastically different than IDEA 1997. Students with disabilities should be part of the regular classroom, as appropriate, with support as needed, unless the nature and severity of the disability requires a more restrictive learning environment.

Schools as "mini-societies" should be supportive of all constituents. Diversity of staff and students should be celebrated. Building leaders should be knowledgeable about all school members. Knowledge of special education transcends all aspects of leadership. Rules and regulation knowledge support students and staff, and the organization. Proactive participation in the eligibility and service delivery process enables building leaders to communicate effectively with students, staff, and parents.

Strategies for alternative instructional techniques and test modifications reinforce options of instruction for *all* students. Teachers focus on accountability issues demanded by curriculum and assessment mandates established by local and state authorities. Sometimes we need to be reminded that the purpose of schools is *for children to learn and develop into members of a democratic society*. Students need to learn information and demonstrate knowledge, not necessarily in a "one-size-fits-all" manner. Teachers need reassurance from building leaders that it is not only permissible, but *preferable* that innovation in teaching and assessment support student success.

Focusing on the following will assist educational leaders in guiding staff to support student success.

CLASSROOM CLIMATE

- Attitudes and perceptions
- Expectations
- Senses of comfort and order
- Respect of self and others
- Responsibility
- Ownership

Teachers need to create a classroom that is a safe, nurturing learning environment for students. Student input is a critical component in establishing class routines and rules. If a teacher asks students what they want in a classroom for themselves, from the teacher, and from and with peers, a trusting relationship can enhance instruction and student success at the K–12 level. Secondary-school students want to feel self-worth in their classrooms. When adults structure activities to allow student input in establishing rules, rewards and consequences, it does not guarantee compliance. Adolescents *test limits* as appropriate developmental steps, but *respect* teachers who respect them. If a student responds outside of established class limits, it is critical to follow through on expected response. This enables students to respect the process they helped establish. Peers will often assist each other in complying with rules in maintaining a sense of fairness for themselves.

Class Vision

The *class vision* should describe what the teacher wants the classroom environment to look like. It must :

- Be clearly communicated
- Serve to direct and inspire students
- State individual and group goals
- Indicate expectations of student and teacher

Benefits of Team Building

There are many educational movements that support team building for staff productivity. The same philosophy works for students in a classroom:

- Greater commitment to the task
- Greater productivity
- More open communication
- Increase of individual growth opportunities
- Higher trust level
- Positive feelings emerge
- More stimulating classroom
- Greater likelihood of successful problem solving
- Respect for group and individual decisions
- Student success

Classroom Organization

Teachers can look at the organization of their classrooms to see whether the environments are conducive to student learning:

- Is the classroom organized for student capacity and appropriate work and study areas?
- Are desks, chairs, and tables at appropriate heights for students?
- Are outside distractions limited?

VISUAL AND AUDITORY ATTENTION

- Do postings on walls and bulletin boards support students' work?
- Are established routines and expectations posted?
- Are reference guides immediately available for students?
- Is the classroom noise level slightly below conversation level?

One aspect that is overlooked in classrooms is the comfort level of students relating to the *physical aspects* of workstations. Students need to be comfortably situated in order to best focus on school tasks. When students are seated, their elbows should be able to rest comfortably on the table or desk, and feet should be on the ground. If a student's chair is too high, feet dangle, allowing fidgeting. The student is not fidgeting because he or she is distracted or impulsive, but because the seating arrangement is inappropriate. Schools often try to raise or lower the heights of desks and tables so that students can reach them, paying little attention to the ability of the student to sit with feet planted firmly on the ground. At the secondary level, desks often have trays for storage under the desk. Tall students cannot fit their legs under the desk and cannot sit correctly. Posture misalignment encourages attention difficulties, because students are forced to put their bodies in a less comfortable position to think, listen, and write. The *best* way for teachers to understand this is for the building leader to have a faculty meeting with inappropriate seating arrangements for staff and a required writing activity. Once staff members are seated, tell them they cannot move or talk. Give them the written task (5–10 minutes), and then ask staff for feedback regarding comfort level. Student seating should be a *priority* in establishing a positive classroom climate.

Establishing ways to realize and recognize student success can be facilitated through the following:

- Learning centers
- Project demonstration
- Plays
- Game making for younger students
- Technology projects
- Computer technology
- Writing
- Community service
- Sports
- Clubs

When school tasks encourage students to complete an activity that helps another student or community member, the meaning drives productivity. Integration of thematic, practical curriculum-driven tasks that can benefit others may include projects that can be consistent with curriculum goals and benefit community members, such as:

TECHNOLOGY

- Students make mercury switches that students with disabilities can use to make toys, TVs, VCRs, and computers start and shut off.
- Build useful tools to do the following:
  - Enable a student with a disability to reach items
  - Assist a student with a disability with eating (using Velcro to keep items in place to increase independence)
  - Assist someone with hearing disability to "see" when someone rings the doorbell by rigging a light bulb to flash on and off.

HOME ECONOMICS

- Include a unit on babysitting issues for students with disabilities
- Make packages for "Meals on Wheels" for elderly community members
- Sew toys for young children (students, hospital patients, homeless youth)

COMPUTERS

- Have students teach homebound seniors how to use e-mail
- Rebuild computers and donate for student use
- Donate software programs no longer used

Coordination of events that students plan for another group within their school community can also build bridges between disabled and non-disabled students. A PTA-sponsored event can be extended to pair students with disabilities with a friend who will attend workshop activities and help students achieve a common goal. This event could take place so that parents of students with disabilities have a shopping day before a holiday, or a respite day to spend time with a sibling of the child with a disability.

SUMMARY

Concepts suggested throughout this book should enable educational leaders to be consumers of special education laws, regulations, concepts, and data. References for day-to-day issues that emerge from staff members, parents, students, and community members have been supplied for a multitude of staff development activities. Professional responsibilities of teachers include maintenance of accurate records, communication with colleagues, parents, administration, participation in school and district initiatives, and continually developing professional goals.

Developing a positive, professional culture in schools and districts should be a vision shared by all educators. The purpose of a professional culture is to enable participation in decision making that benefits student learning (Lieberman, 1988).

Activities for faculty discussed in chapter 5 will create a level of faculty understanding for the educational needs of diverse learners. When educational leaders delegate authority that enables faculty to feel the power of shared decision making at the building level, the educational community benefits. Teachers become more willing to incorporate innovative ideas into teaching practices and teams of teachers will enthusiastically brainstorm ways to develop curricular approaches that enable all students to demonstrate knowledge.

School leaders must develop and facilitate social parameters necessary to achieve shared goals. The goals of schools are for all members of the school community to be valued members. Having the necessary tools to share with staff is an important commodity for building leaders.

When a district philosophy is one of shared decision and site-based management, building-level administrators and teachers are supported and rewarded for their participation in the teaching and learning process. Students strive for that same recognition of worth, and educational leaders that facilitate these concepts build a team of staff members that support *all* students in developing critical thinking skills upon which student learning outcomes are achieved.

REFERENCE RESOURCES FOR PRACTITIONERS

The remainder of this chapter lists resources pertinent to the areas covered in this book. Titles presented focus on practitioners' use of materials, rather than research-oriented materials. You might find the breakdown of resources limited in some areas. Please focus on the content of this book, and understand that all resources listed are helpful in more than one specified area. In fact, listing a resource in one category is only done for the reader's focus for a place to start. The author believes that all resources are cross-categorical.

LEADERSHIP AND CHANGE PROCESS

Aaronsohn, E. (1996). Going against the grain: Supporting the student-centered teacher. Thousand Oaks, CA: Corwin Press.

Brown, J. and Moffett, C. (1999). The hero's journey: How educators can transform schools and improve learning. Alexandria, VA: ASCD.

Byham, Willima C. (1988). Zapp! The lightning of empowerment. New York: Harmony Books.

Fullan, M. (1998). Change forces: Probing the depths of educational reform. New York: Falmer Press.

Fullan, M. and Hargreaves, A. (1996). What's worth fighting for in your school. New York: Teachers College Press.

Iwanicki, E. (1994). Using evaluation to enhance teaching and learning in schools. Paper presented to Nova University National Ed.D. Program for Educational Leaders, Alexandria, VA.

Lutz, F. and Merz, C. (1992). School/Community relations. New York: Teachers College Press.

Moffett, C. (1998, March). Dimensions of learning and the adult learner. Paper presented at the Dimensions Network Forum, San Antonio, Texas.

Sergiovanni, T. (1992). Moral leadership: Getting to the heart of school improvement. San Francisco: Jossey-Bass.

INCLUSION/DIVERSITY

Aefsky, F. (1995). Inclusion confusion: A guide to educating children with exceptional needs. Thousand Oaks, CA: Corwin Press.

Bilken, D. (1992). Schooling without labels: Parents, educators, and inclusive education. Philadelphia: Temple University Press.

Daggert, W. and Kruse, B. (1997). Education is not a spectator sport. Schnectady, NY: Leadership Press.

Gardner, H. (1993). Multiple intelligences: The theory in practice. New York: Basic Books.

Hammeken, P. (1996). An essential guide for the paraprofessional. Minnetonka, MN: Peytral.

Jensen, E. (1998). Teaching with the brain in mind. Alexandria, VA: ASCD.

Klauber, J. and Klauber, A. (1996). Inclusion and parent advocacy: A resource guide. Centereach, NY: Disability Resources.

Kohn, A. (1998). What to look for in a classroom and other essays. San Francisco: Jossey-Bass.

Sapon-Shevin, M. (1999). Because we can change the world: A practical guide to building cooperative, inclusive classroom communities. Needham Heights, MA: Allyn & Bacon.

DISCIPLINE

Hartwig, E. and Ruesch, G. (1994). Discipline in the school. Horsham, PA: LRP Publications.

Honig v. Doe, 479 U.S. 1084, 107 S.Ct. 1284, L. Ed. 2d 142 (1988).

Kohn, A. (1993). Punished by rewards. Boston, MA: Houghton Mifflin.

Nelsen, J., Lott, L., and Glenn, H.S. (1997). Positive discipline in the classroom. Rocklin, CA: Prima.

STANDARDS AND ASSESSMENT

Bradley, D. and Calvin, M. (Nov/Dec 1998). Grading modified assignments: Equity or compromise. *Teaching Exceptional Children*, 24-29.

Marzano, R. and Kendall, J. (1996). Designing standards-based districts, schools and classrooms. Alexandria, VA: ASCD.

Swanson, S. and Howell, C. (1996). Test anxiety in adolescents with learning disabilities and behavior disorders. *Exceptional Children, 62*(5), 389–395.

TEACHER RESOURCES

Armstrong, T. (1994). Multiple intelligences in the classroom. Alexandria, VA: ASCD.

Buck, P. S. (1992). The child who never grew. 2nd ed. Rockville, MD: Woodbine House.

Davis, J. (1995). Interdisciplinary courses and team teaching. Arizona: Oryx Press.

DeMeritt, S. (1995). The overclassification of the American child. *The School Psychologist, 17*(4), 4–19.

Fosnot, C. (1989). Enquiring teachers, enquiring learners: A constructivist approach for teaching. New York: Teachers College Press.

Harmin, M. (1994). Inspiring active learning: A handbook for teachers. Alexandria, VA: ASCD.

Lawton, M. (1999). Co-teaching: Are two heads better than one in an inclusive classroom. *Harvard Education Letter, 15*(2), 1–8.

Marzano. R. (1992). A different kind of classroom: Teaching with dimensions of learning. Alexandria, VA: ASCD.

Price, G. and Dunn, R. (1997). Learning style inventory. Lawrence, KS: Price Systems.

Slavin, R. (1987). Cooperative learning: Student teams. Washington, D.C.: National Education Association.

Slavin, R., Madden, N., Dolan, L., and Wasik, B.(1996). Every child, every school: Success for all. Thousand Oaks, CA: Corwin Press.

Tomlinson, C. (1999). The differentiated classroom: Responding to the needs of all learners. Alexandria, VA: ASCD.

APPENDIX A

Federal Definitions of Disabling Conditions (IDEA 1997)

- **Autism**—a developmental disability affecting verbal, nonverbal communication and socialization significantly, generally evident prior to age three, adversely affecting a child's educational performance. Other characteristics often associated with autism are repetitive activities, resistance to change in routines, and atypical response to sensory and environmental input.
- **Deaf-blindness**—a combination of hearing and visual impairment that causes severe communication and other developmental and educational problems, prohibiting the accommodation in a special education program for children with deafness or blindness.
- **Deafness**—a hearing impairment that severely limits the child's ability to process linguistic information through hearing (with or without amplification), adversely affecting a child's educational performance.
- **Emotional disturbance**—this term means that a student exhibits one or more of the following characteristics over a long period and to a marked degree, which adversely affect the student's educational performance:
  - Inability to learn that cannot be explained by health, sensory, or intellectual factors

- Inability to build or maintain interpersonal relationships with peers or teachers
- Demonstrates inappropriate behavior or feelings under normal circumstances
- Presents a general, pervasive mood of unhappiness or depression
- Has a tendency to develop fears or physical problems associated with personal or school problems

This term does not apply to students who are socially maladjusted, which cannot be attributed to an emotionally disturbed classification, as outlined above.

- **Hearing impairment**—a permanent or fluctuating loss of hearing that adversely impacts a child's ability to learn, but does not meet criteria for deafness.
- **Mental retardation**—significantly subaverage intellectual functioning, existing with deficits in adaptive behavior, manifesting during developmental years, which adversely affects educational performance.
- **Multiple disability**—a combination of two or more significant impairments that causes such severe educational problems that the child's needs cannot be accommodated in special-education programs solely for single impairments, excluding deaf-blindness.
- **Orthopedic impairment**—a severe orthopedic disability, affecting a child's educational performance adversely, including congenital anomalies, impairments caused by disease or other causes, including burns, amputations, cerebral palsy, polio, etc.
- **Other health impairments**—a disability that limits a student's strength, vitality or alertness, due to chronic or acute health problems, including but not limited to a heart condition, tuberculosis, asthma, hemophilia, sickle cell anemia. Children with Attention deficit disorder (ADD) or Attention deficit hyperactivity disorder (ADHD) might be eligible for services under other "health impaired" if the ADD or ADHD is determined

to be a chronic health problem that results in limited alertness, adversely affecting educational performance, and special education and related services are needed because of the ADD or ADHD. The term "limited alertness" includes a child's heightened reaction to environmental stimuli that results in a lack of attention in the educational environment. Note that children with ADD or ADHD might be eligible for special education services under one of the other disability categories if they meet the stated criteria.

- **Specific learning disability**—this is defined as a disorder in one or more of the basic psychological processes involved in understanding or in using language, spoken or written, that manifests in an inability to listen, think, speak, read, write, spell or do mathematical calculations, including conditions such as perceptual disabilities, brain injury, minimal brain dysfunction, dyslexia, or developmental aphasia. Note that this disorder does not include learning problems attributed to visual, hearing, or motor disabilities, mental retardation, emotional disturbance, or environmental, cultural, or economic disadvantage.

- **Speech or language impairment**—a communication disorder such as stuttering, articulation impairment, language or voice impairment, adversely affecting a child's educational performance.

- **Traumatic brain injury**—an acquired (rather than congenital, degenerative, or birth trauma) injury to the brain caused by an external physical force, resulting in total or partial functional disability or psychosocial impairment. Impairments included are the areas of cognition, language, memory, attention, reasoning, abstract thinking, judgment, problem solving, psychosocial behavior, physical functions, processing or speech.

- **Visual impairment**—blindness, partial sight or a vision problem that, even with correction, adversely affects educational performance.

Note: These are the definitions that the Federal Government applies to disabling conditions. Some states have changed disability categories. (For example, in some states "mentally retarded" has become "cognitively delayed"; "autism" has become "pervasive developmental disorder"; and "emotionally disturbed" has become "emotionally handicapped.")

APPENDIX B

There are two basic systems that states use to fund special-need programs. These include *entitlement schemes*: weighting systems, flat grants, individually calculated entitlements and *reimbursement schemes*: excess costs.

Weighting assumes that the cost of providing special services has a fixed relationship to the cost of typical programs (Guthrie, Garms, and Pierce, 1988). A percentage above 100 percent is assigned to various disability categories. Objections to this system have been focused on the possibility that districts might classify students in categories that bring a higher percentage of reimbursement. This system is utilized by 19 states (Parrish, 1997).

Flat grants constitute specified dollar amounts per pupil in special programs (currently in place in ten states). This gives a dollar amount to districts to use in the general category of special programs. Both weighting and flat grants are imprecise, resulting in some districts receiving more and others less than needed to provide services for identified students.

The New Hampshire Supreme Court (12/97) ruled that the state's system of paying for education with property taxes was unconstitutional, because it creates unequal tax burdens (Fattah, 1998). Eighteen other states, including Pennsylvania, New Jersey, Arizona, Connecticut, Indiana, and Ohio are in the process of changing educational financing, with concentrated focus on special education funding issues.

APPENDIX C

Special Education Survey

The information gathered by this survey will be used to compile data for a book to be published.

Position (please check one)

State: ____________

____ principal

____ director

____ assistant superintendent

____ special educator

____ other:

____ assistant principal

____ superintendent

____ parent

____ classroom educator

Concerns in my school (1); district (2); classroom (3); community (4)

Please indicate by respective number all that apply:

____ discipline

____ testing results

____ fairness

____ disruption of instructional process

____ teacher responsibility

____ suspension

____ union issues

____ graduation requirements

____ instructional modifications

____ legal challenges

____ grading

____ resource allocation

____ paperwork

____ equity

____ parental contact

____ compliance

____ curriculum

____ test modifications

____ behavior

____ planning time

These concerns are related to inclusion:

___ yes ___ no ___ some

[If some of the concerns are related to inclusion, indicate those that apply with an asterisk (*).]

Appendix D

Teacher Survey

Years Teaching:
0–5 ____ 6–10 ____ 11+ ____
Regular education ____ Special education ____
Elementary K–1 ____ 2–4 ____ 5–6 ____
Middle School ____ High School ____

Directions: Listed below are various forms of curriculum modifications that some teachers employ for the benefit of students with mild disabilities. For each item, please check whether you use or do not use particular adaptations. If you check do not use, but you would consider doing so given adequate support, please check the third line also. If an item does not apply because of the nature of the subject you teach, check the fourth line.

Curriculum Modifications

Do not use	Would consider using	Does not apply	
_____	_____	_____	1. Provide supplementary content written to a lower readability level than the textbook.
_____	_____	_____	2. Provide alternative textbooks written to a lower readability level.
_____	_____	_____	3. Provide outline of textbook chapters.

Do not use	Would consider using	Does not apply	
_____	_____	_____	4. Provide outlines of lectures.
_____	_____	_____	5. Preview questions and guides for upcoming class discussions.
_____	_____	_____	6. Tape-record content from texts.
_____	_____	_____	7. Provide handouts of transparency overlays.
_____	_____	_____	8. Allow students to tape-record class lectures or discussions.
_____	_____	_____	9. Permit students to independently view films and listen to tapes, outside of class.
_____	_____	_____	10. Highlight the most essential information on handout material.
_____	_____	_____	11. Pair low-ability students with peer tutors for study, review, or test preparation.
_____	_____	_____	12. Allow the student extra time to complete assignments.
_____	_____	_____	13. Administer "practice" tests at the beginning of the semester or new unit.
_____	_____	_____	14. Make out-of-use tests available as study guides.

Do not use	Would consider using	Does not apply	
_____	_____	_____	15. Use alternative tests with simplified readability for poor readers.
_____	_____	_____	16. Allow students with disabilities to tape-record answers to essay questions.
_____	_____	_____	17. Use tape-recorded tests with poor readers.
_____	_____	_____	18. Administer untimed tests outside of class for poor readers and writers.
_____	_____	_____	19. Provide alternative homework assignments for poor readers and writers.
_____	_____	_____	20. During the lesson, allow students with disabilities to work on other assignments.
_____	_____	_____	21. Select fewer concepts for the student to learn, but leave the assignment the same for other students.
_____	_____	_____	22. Place the students in cooperative groups to complete assignments.

Thank You!

APPENDIX E

TABLE 6. MIDDLE SCHOOL SEVENTH- AND EIGHTH-GRADE AVERAGES, 1997

	Midterm grades		Final grades	
	7th	8th	7th	8th
SEIRC students	82.25	81.13	77.5	71.1
All students	85.03	85.70	77.1	75

TABLE 7. MIDDLE SCHOOL SEIRC STUDENT PROFILES, MAY 1997

Range of Scores		
IQ	Reading Achievement	Math Achievement
68 to 118	2.6 to 11.3 g.e.	2.4 to 11.0 g.e.

IQ Scores			
Under 80	80–90	90–109	110–118
4	15	43	4

Average Achievement Scores	
Reading	Math
7.2 g.e.	7.1 g.e.

APPENDIX F

TABLE 8. HIGH SCHOOL COMPARISON OF RANGE OF REPORT CARD GRADES, JANUARY 1998

Subject	SEIRC students	Mainstreamed special ed students	Non-disabled students
Earth Science			
(grade 9)	50–91	50–94	50–94
(2 sections)	71–86	60–87	57–88
English			
(grade 9)	65–83	60–85	54–86
(2 sections)	66–80	20–71	20–76
Global Studies			
(grade 9)	58–93	37–78	52–76
(2 sections)	77–81	65–89	21–86
Math (grade 9)			
(1 section)	67–97	50–88	50–85
English			
(grade 10)	70–95	n/a	56–92
(2 sections)	77–91	82–86	60–95
Biology			
(grade 10)	84–93	81–88	50–100
(2 sections)	80–88	n/a	65–93
Math	17–84	78–89	51–86
(grade 10)	50–85	50–90	67–94
(3 sections)	82–85	77–89	60–97
Global Studies			
(grade 10)	67–79	65–87	60–93
(2 sections)	66–78	72–87	71–95
Math (grade 11)			
(1 section)	55–80	70–90	55–90

APPENDIX G

REFERENCES

Aaronsohn, E. (1996). Going against the grain: Supporting the student-centered teacher. Thousand Oaks, CA: Corwin Press.

Aefsky, F. (1995). Inclusion confusion: A guide to educating children with exceptional needs. Thousand Oaks, CA: Corwin Press.

Armstrong, T. (1994). Multiple intelligences in the classroom. Alexandria, VA: ASCD.

Ayers, G. (1994). Statistical profile of special education in the United States. *Teaching /exceptional Children, 26*(3), 1–4.

Baker, J. and Zigmond, N. (1995). The meaning and practice of inclusion for students with learning disabilities: Themes and implications from the five cases. *Journal of Special Education, 29*(2), 163-80.

Beery, K. (1989). Developmental test of visual-motor integration. Third Ed. Austin, TX: Pro-Ed.

Bender, L. (1938). A visual-motor Gestalt test.

Bilken, D. (1992). Schooling without labels: Parents, educators, and inclusive education. Philadelphia: Temple University Press.

Board of Education of Hendrick Hudson Central School District v. Rowley, 458 U. S. 176, 102 S. Ct. 3034, 73 L. Ed.2d 987, 36 Ed. Law Rep. 1136 (3rd Cir.) (1986).

Bradley, D. and Calvin, M. (Nov/Dec 1998). Grading modified assignments: Equity or compromise. *Teaching Exceptional Children*, 24–29.

Brigance, A. (1980). Brigance inventory of essential skills. North Billerica, MA: Curriculum Associates.

Brown, J. and Moffett, C. (1999). The hero's journey: How educators can transform schools and improve learning. Alexandria, VA: ASCD.

Buck, J. N. (1948). The house-tree-person technique. *Journal of Clinical Psychology, 5.*

Buck, P. S. (1992). The child who never grew. 2nd ed. Rockville, MD: Woodbine House.

Bursuck, W., Polloway, E., Plante, L., Epstein, M., Jayanthi, M., and McConeghy, J. (1996). Report card grading adaptations: A national survey of classroom practices. *Exceptional Children 62*(4), 301–318.

Byham, W.(1988). Zapp: The lightning of empowerment. New York: Harmony Books.

Chaikind, S., Danielson, L., and Brauen, M. (1993). What do we know about the costs of special education: a selected review. *The Journal of Special Education, 26*(4) 344–370.

Connolly, A. J. (1988). KeyMath revised: A diagnostic inventory of essential mathematics. Circle Pines, MN: American Guidance Service.

Culross, R. (Jan/Feb 1997). *Teaching exceptional children.*

Daggert, W. and Kruse, B. (1997). Education is not a spectator sport. Schenectady, NY: Leadership Press.

Daniel R. R. v. State Board of Education, 874 F.2d 1036, 53 Ed. Law Rep. 824 (5th Cir.) (1989).

Darling-Hammond, L. & McLaughlin, M.(1995). Policies that support professional development in an era of reform. Phi Delta Kappan, 597–604.

Davis, J. (1995). Interdisciplinary courses and team teaching. Arizona: Oryx Press.

Deal, T. (1994). *Personnel Psychology, 52*(2), 488–90.

DeMeritt, S. (1995). The overclassification of the American child. *The School Psychologist, 17*(4), 4–19.

Dettmer, P. (1993). Gifted education: Window of opportunity. *Gifted Child Quarterly, 37*(2), 92–94.

DeVries v. Fairfax County School Board, 882 F. 2D 876 (4th Cir.) (1989).

Dunn, R.(1996). How to implement and supervise a learning style program. Alexandria, VA:ASCD.

Education Week. (January 14, 1998). Diverse special education enrollment boosts costs nationwide. 17, 18.

Fattah, C. (1998). A single garment of destiny. *Education Week, 17*(32).

Federal Register: May 6, 1996 (Vol. 61, Number 88). Office of Special Education and Rehabilitative Services. Part 300 Regulations. US Dept. Of Education, Washington, D.C.

Finn, C. (1998). First, do no harm. *Education Week, 17*(32), 52.

Fosnot, C. (1989). Enquiring teachers, enquiring learners: A constructivist approach for teaching. New York: Teachers College Press.

Fullan, M. (1993). Change forces: Probing the depths of educational reform. New York: Falmer Press.

Fullan, M. and Hargreaves, A. (1996). What's worth fighting for in your school. New York: Teachers College Press.

Gardner, H. (1993). Mulitple intelligences: the theory in practice. New York: Basic Books.

Gardner, H. (1995). Leading minds: An anatomy of leadership. New York: Basic Books.

Guthrie, J. W., Garms, W. I., and Pierce, L. (1988). School finance and educational policy. Englewood Cliffs, NJ: Prentice Hall.

Hammeken, P. (1996). An essential guide for the paraprofessional. Minnetonka, MN: Peytral.

Hammill, D. and Larsen, S. (1996). Test of written language-3. Austin, TX: Pro-Ed.

Harmin, M. (1994). Inspiring active learning: A handbook for teachers. Alexandria, VA: ASCD.

Harris, D. B. (1963). Goodenough-Harris drawing test. New York: Harcourt Brace Jovanovich.

Hartmann v. Loudoun County (1997). US Court of Appeals, 4th Cir. Fed Sup 3rd.

Hartwig, E. and Ruesch, G. (1994). Discipline in the school. Horsham, PA: LRP Publications.

Holland decision keeps cost an unlikely factor in special education cases. 1994. *The Special Educator, 9*, 189–190.

Holmes, N. (1998). Fully fund special education, AASA urges Congress, as IDEA work begins. http://www.aasa.org/Latest/latest/39.htm.

Honig v. Doe, 479 U.S. 1084, 107 S.Ct. 1284, L. Ed. 2d 142 (1988).

Hopkins, K. (1998). Educational and psychological measurement and evaluation. Needham Heights, MA: Allyn & Bacon.

Hunter, M. (1984). Knowing, teaching and supervising. In *Using what we know about teaching*, edited by P. Hosford (1984 Yearbook). Alexandria, VA: ASCD.

Iwanicki, E. (1994). Using evaluation to enhance teaching and learning in schools. Paper presented to Nova University National Ed.D. Program for Educational Leaders, Alexandria, VA.

Jackson, N. E. (1993). Moving into the mainstream: Reflections on the study of giftedness. *Gifted Child Quarterly, 37*(1), 46-50.

Jacobs, H.H. (Ed.). (1989). Interdisciplinary curriculum: Design Implementation. Alexandria, VA: ASCD.

Jensen, E. (1998). Teaching with the brain in mind. Alexandria, VA: ASCD.

Johnson, D. and Johnson, R. (1987). Creative conflict.Edina, MN: Interaction Book Company.

Johnston, R. (1997). Michigan resolves debate on special education funding. *Education Week, 17*(13), 12–15.

Jordan, T. (1997). The interaction of shifting special education policies with state funding practices. *Journal of Educational Finance, 12*(1) 43–68.

Kentta, B. (1997). The central role in shared decision making. *School Administrator, 54,*(3), 24–26,28; March 1997.

Kilgore, K. & Webb, R. (1997). *Middle School Journal, 28,* May 1997, 3–13.

Kniep, M. (1995). Designing schools and curriculums for the 21st century. ASCD Yearbook. Alexandria, VA: ASCD.

Kohn, A. (1998). What to look for in a classroom and other essays. San Francisco: Jossey-Bass.

Kohn, A. (1993). Punished by rewards. Boston: Houghton Mifflin.

Lawton, M. (1999). Co-teaching: Are two heads better than one in an inclusive classroom. *Harvard Education Letter, 15*(2), 1–8.

Lieberman, A. (1988). Building professional culture in schools. Edited. New York: Teachers College Press.

Lortie, D. (1975). Schoolteacher: A sociological study. Chicago: University of Chicago Press.

Lotir, D. (1975). Schoolteacher: A sociological study. Chicago: University of Chicago Press.

Lutz, F. and Merz, C. (1992). School/Community relations. New York: Teachers College Press.

Machover, K. (1949). Personality projections in the drawing of the human figure. Springfield, IL: C. C. Thomas.

Maker, C. J. (1995). Teaching models in the education of the gifted. Austin, TX: Pro-Ed.

Marzano, R. (1992), A different kind of classroom: Teaching with dimensions of learning. Alexandria, VA: ASCD.

Marzano, R. and Kendall, J. (1996). Designing standards-based districts, schools and classrooms. Alexandria, VA: ASCD.

Marzano. R. (1992). A different kind of classroom: Teaching with dimensions of learning. Alexandria, VA: ASCD.

Mckenna, B. (1998). Change: Some assumptions, theories, models and propositions. Presentation at Monroe-Woodbury Central School District summer Institute, July 24th.

Meek, A., ed. (1995). Designing places for learning. Alexandria, VA: ASCD.

Merenbloom, E. (1996). Team teaching: Addressing the learning needs of middle level students. *NASSP Bulletin, 80* (578), 45–53.

Miles, M. B. (1965). Planned change and organizational health: Figure and ground. In Oregon state position paper, *Change Process in Public Schools.* Mills, R. (28 May 1998). Special education: It's time to act. New York School Boards. 11.

Moffett, C. (March 1998). Dimensions of learning and the adult learner. Paper presented at the Dimensions Network Forum, San Antonio, Texas.

Munk, D. and Bursuck, W. (January 1998). Can grades be helpful and fair? *Educational Leadership*, 44–47.

Murray. H. (1943), Thematic Apperception Test. Cambridge, MA: Harvard University.

Naglieri, J. (1994). Draw a person: Screening for emotional disturbance. Brandon, VT: Clinical Psychology Publishing Company.

National Middle School Association (1995). This we believe. Columbus, Ohio.

Nelsen, J., Lott, L., and Glenn, H.S. (1997). Positive discipline in the classroom. Rocklin, CA: Prima.

New York State Board of Regents. (1998). Proposal on school aid. Albany: The University of the State of New York, State Education Department.

Oberti v. Board of Education of Clementon School District, 995 F. Supp. 1204 (E.D. N.J.) (1993).

Overton, T. (1992). Assessment in special education. Englewood Cliffs, NJ: Prentice Hall.

Parrish, T. (1997). Special education in an era of school reform: Special education finance. Washington, DC: Federal Resource Center.

Price, G. and Dunn, R. (1997). Learning style inventory. Lawrence, KS: Price Systems.

Rotter,J. and Rafferty,J(1950). The Rotter incomplete sentences test. New York: Psychological Corporation.

Sacramento City Unified School District v. Holland, No. 92-15608, (9th Cir.) (1994).

Sapon-Shevin. (1999). Because we can change the world: A practical guide to building cooperative, inclusive classroom communities. Needham Heights, MA: Allyn & Bacon.

Sergiovanni, T. (1992). Moral leadership: Getting to the heart of school improvement. San Francisco: Jossey-Bass.

Sergiovanni, T.J. (1996). Leadership for the schoolhouse: How is it different? Why is it important? 1st ed. San Francisco: Jossey-Bass.

Sergiovanni, T. J. and Starrett, R. J. (1983). Supervising human perspectives. New York: McGraw-Hill.

Shapiro, E. (1996). Academic skills problems. New York: Guilford Press.

Sizer, T. (1991). No pain, no gain. *Educational Leadership, 48* (8), 32–34.

Skrtic, T. (1991). The special education paradox: Equity as the way to excellence. *Harvard Educational Review, 61*(2), 148–206.

Slavin, R. (1986). *American Educator: The Professional Journal of the American Federation of Teachers, 10*(2) 6–11. Summer.

Slavin, R., Madden, N., Dolan, L., and Wasik, B.(1996). Every child, every school: Success for all. Thousand Oaks, CA: Corwin Press.

Sparks, D. and Loucks, S. (1989). Five models of staff development for teachers. *Journal of Staff Development, 10*(4), 40–55.

Sparrow, S., Balla, D., and Chicchetti, D. (1984). Vineland Adaptive Scales. Circle Pines, MN: American Guidance Service.

Swanson, S. and Howell, C. (1996). Test anxiety in adolescents with learning disabilities and behavior disorders. *Exceptional Children, 62*(5), 389–395.

Thorndike, R., Hagan, E., and Satttler, J. (1986). Stanford-Binet intelligence scale. 4th ed. Chicago: Riverside Publishing Company.

Tomlinson, C. (1999). The differentiated classroom: Responding to the needs of all learners. Alexandria, VA: ASCD.

U.S. Department of Education. 1993b). The national education goals report 1: Building a nation of leaders. Washington, DC: Author (Will, M.).

Vavrus, L. (1990). Put portfolios to the test. *Instructor, 100*(1), 48–53.

Villa, R., Thousand, J., Stainbeck,W., and Stainbeck, S. (1992). Restructuring for caring and effective education. Baltimore, MD: Brooks Publishing.

Wechsler, D. (1991). Wechsler intelligence scale for children. 3rd ed. San Antonio, TX: Psychological Corporation.

Weiderholt,L. and Bryant,B.(1992). Gray Oral Reading Test-3. Austin, TX: Pro-ed.

Wesson, C. and King, R. (1996). Portfolio assessment and special education students. *Teaching Exceptional Children*, Winter.

Wiles, J. W. (1993). Promoting change in schools. New York: Scholastic.

Woodcock, R. W. (1987). Woodcock reading mastery test. Revised. Circle Pines, MN: American Guidance Service.

Woodcock, R. W. and Johnson, M. (1989). Woodcock-Johnson tests of achievement. Allen, TX: DLM Teaching Resources.

Ysseldyke, J, & Fox, N. (1997). Implementing inclusion at the middle school level: Lessons from a negative example. *Exceptional Children, 64*(1), 81–98.